THE

UNDERWATER

WORLD

THE UNDERWATER WORLD

A Complete Guide to Diving,
Spearfishing, and Other
Underwater Secrets

by John Tassos

PRENTICE-HALL, INC.
Englewood Cliffs, N. J.

LIBRARY OF CONGRESS CATALOG CARD NUMBER 57–5557

First printing..............*March, 1957*
Second printing........*November, 1960*

PRINTED IN THE UNITED STATES OF AMERICA

93570–S

This Book Is Tenderly Dedicated
To My Two Redheads

〜〜〜〜〜〜〜〜〜〜〜〜〜〜〜〜〜

Alie's first catch was a baby thresher shark
and Penny has yet to whet her taste
for fishing waters.

Preface

I HAD FASHIONED MY FIRST SPEAR from a discarded red broom handle to which I had nailed a twin-tined spearhead. Thus armed, and wearing an early face mask that chafed more than it should have, I dove ten feet to the bottom of a hole in the shallows of the lower Florida Keys. Lobsters were everywhere—I had seen them on an earlier dive. That was what had led me to fashion my first underwater weapon.

On that day, nine years ago, I speared my first lobster for myself; my cocker, Lady Bunny II; and for Bunny's adopted alley kitten from Key West, Conch I. I speared clumsily. The first five thrusts missed their targets. Lobsters tailed it back into the crevices of the jagged coral rock. But many dives later I came up with three lobsters and, on the beach in front of the home I had built on one of the deserted islands, my animals and I dined royally on lobster thermidor, conch salad, and iced tea.

Since those early diving days I have visited California, Cuba, the Bahamas, Haiti, Puerto Rico, Curaçao, Panama, and most of South America—many of the better diving areas of the Western Hemisphere. In each of them I saw an ever-increasing number of underwater divers. On one beach in the Bahamas I counted more underwater devotees than surface swimmers.

The underwater seems to leave its enthusiasts breathless, not only after the first dive but after subsequent dives too. Much has been written about the feeling of the underwater: like walking on clouds . . . like being on Mars . . . like being in a void . . . breathtaking joy with no inhibitions. All these and many more impressions strike you the first time under. But it takes many more dives really to feel and understand the meaning of being with, under, and a part of the water.

When you've left the water and find yourself lying awake in bed dreaming of underwater chills and mysteries, feeling the urge to seek more, imagining encounters with sharks and morays and octopuses—then, and only then, are you truly a captive of skin diving, a dyed-in-the-brine fan.

This book tells how to survive under the water. It is meant for light, not studious, reading. It introduces a new fan to the rights and wrongs of underwater existence. To the veteran it should be a reminder that the water, no matter how inviting and thrilling, contains some elements of danger.

The reader will find stories scattered through the book, some mine, some drawn from other divers' experiences. Some are on the rough side, and others are amusing. And this is as it should be, for the water is just as capable of being cruel as kind, cold as warm, comfortable as terrifying. But it is always fascinating—and, for many of us, irresistible.

Table of Contents

THE
Underwater
World

The Call of the Underwater

IN ALL MAN'S THOUSANDS OF YEARS on earth he has not gone very far.

Not far, that is, above or below the surface of the earth. The outer limits of man's most advanced exploration have been pushed only sixteen miles up and two and a half miles down from the friendly skin of the globe we inhabit. Those are records: the vast majority of us go only as high as a commercial plane flies, as deep, perhaps, as a swan dive. In this fact lies the greatest appeal of the underwater: to quit man's proper sphere and enter another—the world of the fish and the sea plants.

SKIN DIVING UNLOCKS A NEW WORLD

It is a comparatively new world for man, and a challenging one. We can climb a mountain or fly a few thousand feet into the air and nothing much happens. The world is still the same one, recognizable and familiar, and the air breathes about the same. But only ten feet below the surface of the water man is where he does not belong. He can't breathe, although the fish around him can. He is squeezed and, at the same time, buoyed up by pressures suddenly vastly greater than on the surface. Objects appear different, colors and light play strange tricks. Man is a visitor and can only stay a short time.

The object of all the preparation, all the equipment, all the training that goes into underwater activities is to extend that stay, to make it as comfortable and convenient as possible for man, the mammal, to act like a fish.

The most important key that first opens the underwater to man is an underwater mask. Without it our eyes see poorly under water—just a blurred approximation of reality. But strap on a face mask and look down from below the surface, and suddenly you have made the great breakthrough. For the very first time you have truly *seen* in the water. There are colors you have never imagined possible, distinct shapes, gentle movements, flickering light. To the mask, add a snorkel —a short breathing tube you grasp in your teeth. Its end sticks up above the surface a little, and with it you can forget about raising your head to breathe. You can look longer and see more. To extend the range still further, go web-footed by putting on a pair of rubber flippers, and with them, swim faster and with far less conscious effort.

INTERESTS ABOUND BELOW THE SURFACE

Actually, to be like a fish you have to be able to get down into the water and stay a while, below the surface. There is breathing equipment to let you do just that. With a mechanical breathing lung on your back you are finally free of all the old restrictions. Then you find out what it's all about.

Sight-seeing. Practically weightless, you hang suspended in the water. A wave of the arms and you rise gently. A flip of the toes and you glide effortlessly in any direction. A gentle spring from the bottom and you "climb" a fifteen-foot underwater cliff. Then you begin to understand the skin diver's fanaticism. All about you are sights unlike any you have seen before. In a blue-green world there are coral towers like giant mushroom stems, conches that carry their houses on their backs, tiny palm trees that aren't palm trees at all, but really living animals, multi-colored sea fans swaying gravely in the current, octopuses changing their color in anger, and blowfish pumping themselves up in fear. There before your face is a three-pound snapper, looking far different than he would on the dinner table or even gasping at the end of an angler's line. Thousands of tiny, brightly-colored tropical fish flit by; the grunts swim up to your facepiece and peer in, and if you squint, they dash for cover. Far above, the surface of the water is a shimmering greyish ceiling.

There is enough to look at under the seas—even in the relatively tiny proportion of water shallow enough for man to penetrate—to keep one occupied for a lifetime. Many skin divers are merely content to exist in the water and look, and well they may be. But one of the fine things about underwater activities is the tremendous range of interests, one related to the other, that branch out from the central fact of "making like" a fish.

Spearfishing. Chief among these, of course, is spearfishing. This is to surface fishing what stalking a tiger on foot through the jungle with a knife is to shooting prairie dogs from a low-flying helicopter with a 16-gauge shotgun. The hunter is on as near equal terms with his prey as it is possible to get. As a matter of fact, except for man's superior weapons and brain, the fish has the advantage. He's certainly a better swimmer, his body is made to stand the temperatures and pressures, and he doesn't have to worry about compressed air tanks, face mask, or holding his breath.

As a result, many known fish become good sport fish to the skin diver. A fish like the mackerel, for example, fair game for an angler, too, is plenty challenging when you try to aim a spear at his silvery flash. Bigger fish are easier to hit, but wresting a ten-pound grouper or a two-hundred pound jewfish from inside his coral lair takes both strength and skill. And when you tangle with characters like sharks or barracudas or manta rays—well, there's a tingly feeling that it's you or them. The larger 'cudas and most sharks are easily equipped to tear apart a human diver.

Photography. If spearfishermen are the most fanatic of underwater devotees, underwater photographers run a good second best. Anyone who knows something about taking pictures on the surface can learn how to be at home in the water and then find out about the specific problems and techniques of shooting pictures through water instead of air. It's like photography anywhere, but much more challenging and unpredictable.

There are many levels of underwater photography, starting just below the surface. With a special plastic case even a box camera can take a snapshot of the kids porpoising through shallow water. More elaborate camera boxes, pressurized and fitted with exterior controls, will take professional cameras and intricate lighting attachments deep under the surface, where the sudden lighting of a flash bulb illumines fish and plants and rocks of uncannily beautiful colors—colors that were there all the time but have never before been struck by light and thus revealed.

Wreck exploration. Another side hobby for underwater fans is wreck exploration. What could be more intriguing than a dead ship, lying on its side deep in the sand or silt, encrusted with coral and overgrown with sea plants? Divers going down to investigate sometimes come upon an octopus haunting once gay dining salons, and others collect lobster dinners, clustered in battered superstructures.

Collecting shells. In contrast to the massive hulks of ships are the fragile shells one finds in the sea. Once a collector fits a mask to his face for an undersurface dive, he will hunt shells no other way. Abandoned shells are common enough on the beaches, where they are washed up by tides. But there they are battered and crushed and picked over by shell collectors. On the bottom, shells are the homes of living animals that one must chase to catch. The colors and forms are perfect and clear.

SCIENCE TAKES A LOOK

Serious scientists, as well as sportsmen, find a new frontier for exploration by means of improved shallow-water breathing devices and the diving lung. With today's underwater equipment not exceeding three hundred dollars per diver, geologists, archaeologists, biologists, and ichthyologists are diving to the ocean's bottom to learn at first hand what the sea has been sheltering these millions of years.

Each scientist discovers new vistas opening for him underwater. The geologist, who studies the history of the earth and its life as revealed in rock formation, now sees rock formations underseas, the same sort that moulded the mountains and valleys on earth. And these geologist-divers are learning that the three principal land studies of geology—the geotonic, dynamic, and historic—are also keen subjects for study underwater.

Because one of the primary functions of the geologist today is hunting for petroleum, the sea takes on new significance with the discovery of "offshore" oil fields. The geologist has donned mask, flippers, and breathing lung to study rock formations, to take samples which determine the age of the rocks, and to seek fossil and other structures that offer clues to existence of oil pools over vast submerged land areas. With this gear he is discovering oil deposits in the Gulf of Mexico, California waters, the Persian Gulf, and other locations.

Biologists too, studying and reporting on the science of life itself, now take advantage of new underwater equipment to observe life and living beings in their natural habitat. No longer must they completely rely upon laboratory examination of specimens.

One favorite haunt of the underwater research scientist is the famous Lerner Marine Laboratory on the island of Bimini in the Bahamas. Here, hundreds of men and women from universities and institutions the world over periodically gather to study. What is being reported by these scientists? Volumes of their printed works include such specialized reports as: eye implantation in fish (by a neurologist); social behavior of fish; how fish can stand the crushing pressures of the deep, yet are able to rise to the lesser pressures of shallow waters; studies in fish locomotion; and hundreds of other studies, all, in varying degrees, enlarging the science of underwater biology.

Invading the watery kingdom too, are the ichthyologists, biologists who specialize in the study of fish. Until recently, a systematical charting of fish life has been virtually unknown. Now, with air breathing tanks strapped to their backs, enthusiastic ichthyologists surface with credible reports of what actually happens below the surface.

Laden with slate boards around his waist, the scientist spends hours sitting on the bottom or swimming among the coral and observing the habits of all sea life, including sea urchins, sea cucumbers that squirt harmless fluids, and angel fish that busy themselves all day long around their reef home. He may try to make friends with the voracious barracuda by feeding him conch, offered at the end of a spear shaft.

Frank Trevor, biology instructor from the Millbrook School in New York, and his associate, Roswell Miller of Nassau and Millbrook, were able to accomplish the transfer of a rare species of tropical fish known as Fairy Bass (tiny purple and gold fish, capable of swimming forward, backward, up and down, and sideways), and became the first persons to make possible the survival of these fish outside their natural habitat.

As the ichthyologist pieces together information on the habits and the life of fish, so the archaeologist pieces together the history of the ages by studying fossil remains, internments, inscriptions, and relics. Today, divers are doing the work of archaeologists by donning portable diving gear to dive back into chapters of history that the seas have successfully concealed for centuries. Divers are discovering relics of the civilizations of seafaring cultures like Greece, Phoenicia, Palestine, and Canaan on the ocean floor, buried under ever-building deposits of mud, fish skeletons, and other sediments, in some instances, a hundred or more feet deep.

The first archaeological triumph occurred in 1901 in the waters of the Island of Antikythera, off the coast of Greece. A Greek sponge ship captain, seeking refuge from a storm, accidentally discovered marble and bronze statues of the Periclean Age, which are presently on exhibit at the National Museum.

One of the truly great undersea discoveries that contributed to piecing together fragments of history was recently found in 127 feet of water off the coast of Tunisia, near the Arabian town of Mahdia. Exploration from 1907 to 1913 brought to the surface preciously preserved Greek columns, capitals, marble blocks, anchors, storage amphorae for wine and food, busts, and bronze carvings. This treasure, the second important undersea archaeological find, was traced to Greece in the first century. The experts pieced together the story: The vessel, a cargo sailing ship, looted the Greek port of Athens for the Roman Dictator Lucius Cornelius Sulla (B.C. 138–78), who was then on a circuiting warring tour of Greece and Asia Minor. Ironically enough, Greek divers, easily the best deep sea divers in the world, were employed by the Tunisian government to bring back to our civilization the treasures that once belonged to their ancestors.

In 1948, Captain J. Y. Cousteau, French underseas explorer and co-inventor of the Aqua-Lung, with his crew sought out the Mahdia treasure ship. They dug into the seabed to discover leaden plates of the deck, Ionic capitals, bronze nails, and a cedar rib that was still covered with a marine varnish that had survived the salt water for twenty centuries. In his book, *The Silent World*, Cousteau indicates that much of the original cargo is probably still in the hold, and the ship, estimated to be 130 feet in length with a 40-foot beam, is probably buried far beneath the sea's alluvial deposits.

THE ANCIENT BEGINNINGS AND THE DEVELOPMENT OF THE SPORT

The specialties of the undersea are innumerable. But the real impact of underwater addiction is a more universal thing, a basic appeal that drives thousands of week-end skin divers into the sea with never a thought of discovering oil or tangling with a sea monster, no interest at all in the sex life of a vestlet. They are attracted primarily by the dramatic fact that they have learned how to go where man is not accustomed to going, to a realm where it is quite possible for a neophyte to see candelabra coral, or walk upon a stretch of ocean floor never before beheld, much less trod, by a human. The mystery is impressive. The seas have been there, with their billions of inhabitants, so very long. This is where life began many geological ages before there was even vegetation on our land.

Over the ages relatively few men have gone into the deep waters; men have always been somewhat afraid of the sea and have told fearsome stories about it. But fish have been speared for thousands of years, usually in shallow water. Ancient peoples of the Mediterranean and the Far East learned to dive for food, pearls, and sponges, and their descendants are still doing it today.

To trace the development of underwater activity, one merely turns to the pages of history. Homer referred to divers of the sea in his epic *The Iliad*, and Aristotle reported on underwater diving, too.

Great ancient generals employed divers, although their equipment is not described, to destroy enemy harbor installations; and Xerxes of Persia was known to use Greek divers to recover gold and other treasures from sunken ships. Italy's Leonardo da Vinci, the Florentine painter known for his famous "Mona Lisa," was also an engineer and inventor who worked with underwater breathing devices. Divers are mentioned everywhere in history. The twelfth century reveals many, and still earlier, the Dravidians of the East were known to have mastered underwater ship repair on their trading vessels. Later, some of the modern day pioneers of the early nineteenth century got on the diving track by working with watertight dress made of goatskin.

Deep diving equipment was developed only during the nineteenth century, and is still used for heavy deep sea work. But the helmet, leaded shoes, and dress are clumsy, and the diver is tied by air and life lines to the surface. Self-contained equipment, the second key to acting like a fish, has been developed in this century. The growth of spearfishing as a sort of French Riviera fad just before World War II, combined with development during the war of a compressed air breathing lung by Captain J. Y. Cousteau and Émile Gagnan, a French engineer, and Cousteau's associates of the French Navy, gave underwater sport its first real spurt.

Diving for pearls and shells by natives of Australia, New Guinea, and the islands of the South Pacific, and for sponge by Greek divers in the Mediterranean and at Tarpon Springs, Florida, brought records of deep dives exceeding 120 and even 160 feet without the use of breathing devices. French,

Polynesian, British, Italian—natives of almost every country with a seacoast—went for deep-water dives of sorts, some accurately recorded and others hearsay. Their very existence, accurate or otherwise, attests to the popularity and interest of the underwater. Earlier documentation, at best, is spotty. Underwater interests were secondary to those of navigation and shipping. Those interested in underwater activity were scattered with no central organization.

There were a handful of skin divers in the United States at the end of World War II. Now, in areas with good diving waters, like those of California, Florida, and the Caribbean, skin diving and spearfishing have become major forms of recreation. Resort hotels offer underwater tours and spearfishing facilities. Schools have sprung up to teach diving techniques. Diving and fishing equipment have become important stock items in sporting goods stores. Books, motion pictures, and magazines are devoted to the field. There are, today, some 420 underwater clubs with thousands of members organized to enjoy and promote good practices in the water. One out of every ten swimmers in the country, it is estimated, owns at least one piece of diving equipment. And at least one man looking for a homesite in Florida insisted on swimming offshore from each property he inspected; he would not buy where there was not good fishing water for his underwater hobby.

Another enterprising businessman in Miami advertises his underwater equipment on a billboard located on the ocean bottom, off Key Largo in the Florida Keys.

As a sport, underwater diving has a recent history. The most important link in its world acclaim and recognition as a profession, before underwater activity became a sport, came during World War II. The American Underwater Demolition Teams (UDT) used the underwater crafts and skills to spearhead amphibian landings by blasting enemy beach installations to make a safe approach for their invading units. This offensive action was not original with the U.S.A. Early in history, during the reign of Alexander the Great, King of Macedon, this shrewd strategist had divers trained to demolish underwater barriers on the shores of the biblical city of Tyre. Frogmen, as the contemporary underwater armed forces experts are popular known, made war history in their advance operations on the beaches of Normandy, the Marshall Islands, Guam, and Borneo. Other countries trained underwater demolition experts, too. The Italians had been perfecting artificial breathing equipment and used it successfully with a two-man underwater craft at the heavily-protected Gibraltar Harbor in September, 1941. English frogmen swam ashore in the Dieppe raid, and Japanese underwater experts were used to clear the beaches at Hong Kong.

Servicemen in all parts of the world who had a taste of underwater activity were, to a large measure, responsible for popularizing the sport following World War II. European ex-servicemen took to the Rivieras of France and Italy with mask and fins and later with breathing lungs. Harpoons and spearguns were fashioned, and the march toward a new and exciting sport was under way. The European exploits were soon told to masses of adventurers in Florida, California, the Gold Coast, the Great Lakes, the inland lakes, the northeast Atlantic and northwest Pacific coastlines. The cult spread to Hawaii and into the Caribbean among the scattered vanguards who, even before World War II, had already penetrated the waters with primitive mask, fin, and harpoon.

The motion picture studios in Hollywood were quick to

make feature-length films centered about skin diving and the underwater. *The Frogmen*, the first major production, was soon followed by *Under the Twelve Mile Reef*. Both films came from the Twentieth Century Fox lot, the latter directed by veteran adventurer Bob Webb. Box office successes prompted the production of Jules Verne's *Twenty Thousand Leagues Under the Sea*. RKO followed in the briny success with a feminine excursion below the depths, appropriately entitled *Underwater*, starring the well-proportioned Jane Russell, who looked good even in an Aqua-Lung. Two documentaries, both well presented, had further effect on Americans starved for new adventure: *Under the Red Sea*, a drama of underwater life in color, was filmed under the direction of Austrian Hans Haas, a veteran diver who first glimpsed the revelations of the undersea on the French Riviera with writer-fisherman Guy Gilpatrick. *Hunters of the Deep*, another documentary in color, was a release by several underwater cameramen who independently toured the Caribbean and the Pacific. Some of its photographers were members of the famed Scripps Institute of Oceanography and the Hancock Institute of Los Angeles.

The humor of Americans will always be present, whether on the stage or in business or underwater. The UDT men of the Pacific left an insulting trademark for the well-publicized U.S. Marines. On an island installation, a sign reading, "Beaches cleared for the U.S. Marines through the courtesy of UDT—USO two blocks to the right," was alleged to have been erected under Japanese fire, immediately after clearing landing facilities with dynamite.

And one of the happiest men I know has really made the underwater a part of his regular life. He has a nagging wife.

Weighted down with extra lead and wearing a double-tank compressed-air lung, he likes to drift down to a sandy bottom, curl up, and nap for two hours. This may be a perversion of the sport, but my friend has a sandbag for a pillow and enjoys a quiet, unknown on the surface. When he finally emerges from the water—only, I suspect, because he is out of air—he has a satisfied grin on his face.

2

What's in the Sea

THERE IS PLENTY OF PLAYING FIELD for the underwater sportsman, a vast laboratory for the inquisitive.

Of the 196,950,000 square miles of the earth's surface, 139,440,000 square miles—more than 70 per cent—are covered by the seas. That's a lot of water—in volume, about 323,-722,000 cubic miles. Considering only the small slice of water relatively near the surface that a skin diver can penetrate, the underwater fan has plenty of space—more than all the mountain climber's mountains, all the "spelunker's" caves, the hunter's jungles, and sports car enthusiast's racetracks; more than all the baseball diamonds and football fields and chess clubs in the world.

Of course, man has explored only a small fraction of the world's water. And some of the dark corners of the sea will never be penetrated by man's fragile body; the depths are too great, the pressures too crushing. Such deep cavities as the Marianas Trench off the Philippines—6.8 miles deep—would crush the stoutest vessel that men have devised to carry them where they cannot go unprotected. Of all man's inventions, only the invisible beams of electronic sounding devices have penetrated the ultimate depths.

Even with a mechanical lung, the diver is limited to perhaps the first two hundred feet of the ocean depths, the safe boundary—except for specially trained record-setters and experienced skin divers. But, fortunately, it is the surface waters of the globe that are most wonderfully rich in life and movement. It is here that most sea plants grow, here that different kinds of jellyfish float. In these surface waters most of the familiar fish live and die, and on the shallow bottoms, minute sea organisms build their coral homes.

WHAT MAKES AN OCEAN?

The sea is mostly H_2O, of course—hydrogen and oxygen. The free oxygen in it supports life just as it does on the surface. But whereas man and the other surface creatures breathe oxygen by passing air through their lungs, the fish "breathe" it by taking in water through their mouths, extracting the oxygen they need and expelling the water through their gills.

Ocean water is full of a great many things. It contains iodine, potash, sulphur, bromine, gold, and silver. Almost all the elements have been identified in sea water, although most are present in only minute traces. Some substances such as borax, gypsum, phosphates, magnesium, and common salt are present in large enough amounts to be recovered commercially.

Everyone knows the ocean is salty. Why? Primarily—of all things—because of fresh water. Day after day, millenium after millenium, mountain streams, lakes, and rivers send their water eventually to the sea. The water is "fresh," but it contains small amounts of salts, mostly common sodium chloride or table salt. The salt content of the oceans has built up over the ages until now there are more than one hundred and sixty million tons of salts in a cubic mile of sea water. There is enough salt in the ocean to supply all the world's need for approximately one hundred thousand years! Some seas are saltier than others; in some of the great inland seas, where evaporation is high, the salt content is so great that no fish can live in it. The Dead Sea is one such body of water. The waters of the Polar regions, on the other hand, are less salty than average, because the constant melting of ice and snow pours a lot of relatively salt-less fresh water into them. The average salt content of the Atlantic Ocean is about 34.5 parts per thousand.

Fresh water, entering the ocean, is lighter than salt water, and the great rivers' inflow can be traced for quite a distance. At the mouths of powerful rivers like the Mississippi, the Nile, and the Ob-Irtish, fresh water can sometimes be scooped from the ocean's surface as far out as one hundred miles. Slowly, the stream of fresh water breaks up and loses its identity, becoming one with the salted seas.

Water, seemingly so fragile in small quantities, is a mighty force in large amounts. It provides the roadways for great fleets that maintain world trade. It seems empty and desolate, but actually contains billions of tiny particles of vegetable and mineral matter that form the basis of its whole scheme of life.

Water is, in itself, almost colorless, but it supports the complete register of colors as brilliant as those on the surface. Every known color of the spectrum has been identified in the seas. These colors cannot be discerned much below two hundred feet, for sunlight does not usually penetrate so deeply; but artificial light discovers colors at far greater depths.

During the recent Calypso Oceanographic Expeditions, which resulted in the filming of Captain Cousteau's *The Silent World*, a new record for photoflood lighting was established at 237 feet. True registry of all colors was photographed with specially designed 6000 watt bulbs at this remarkable depth. This proved, again, that color does exist at extreme depths but is invisible to the naked eye. The coral wall that Cousteau photographed was alive with colors. Reds and yellows were as vivid as reds and yellows seen on the surface. Color splashed its glitter as though happy to show it—and for the first time, someone recorded it at such a depth by the use of photoflood light.

A LESSON IN GEOGRAPHY

The sea has a geography of its own. As the surface world has mountains and valleys and plateaus, so does the sea. The skin diver who enters the ocean and examines the floor will see mountains and hills, plateaus and ridges, steep ravines and sharp gorges. In shallow water, these ups and downs are covered with plant life, and the diver sees fish dart in and out of caves and crevices, much as land animals move over the landscape. But in the water the diver floats almost effortlessly up and down one-hundred-foot rock faces. He can pluck a hydroid from such mountainsides much more easily than a climber picks edelweiss from an Alpine slope.

How did the ocean happen? No one is sure, for it was a long time ago. But scientists think it all began with rain—rain that fell for thousands of years when the earth was a slowly cooling mass of what had been molten rock and metal. The rain filled the low parts, and then there were oceans. Over the millenia, the sea's level rose and fell as the earth shivered and crinkled in seismic convulsions, and as alternating cold and hot eras built polar caps that advanced and then receded. At times, when the glaciers covered much of the earth and piled the water up in solid walls, much of what is now ocean was solid land. Then the glaciers receded, and water covered mountains higher than Everest. On the other hand, the marks of what were once seas are left today on what we know as land; oil deposits and limestone, deserts and sedimentary rock are all indications that ancient seas once paid a visit.

The skin diver who leaves the surface to enter the underwater world should know something of the sea's own climate, the changing conditions that govern life—including, temporarily, his own.

Currents. The oceans, first of all, react to surface winds. Wind, or air in motion, affects the temperature of the water it passes over as it does that of the land, and the strength and direction of the winds affect the surface of the water. A brisk wind raises a choppy sea; a heavy gale piles up the waves into sixty-foot-high battering rams and sends them chasing across to the nearest continent. Skin divers do not go exploring in hurricanes, even though the surface turmoil of a storm is not as evident in the water under the surface. If a storm comes up, it can often be weathered more safely underwater than on the surface.

The sea has its own kind of "winds"—the currents—which underwater divers learn to know and to treat with respect. Tremendous amounts of water are moved by the set of the currents along paths that the sea knows as well as a commuter knows the way to work, and which the sea has been following through all recorded history. A current has speed and width and depth, too. It does not involve all the water in a vertical slice of the ocean, but is limited to certain levels by variations in temperature, density, salinity, and the tidal action of sun and moon. Some currents, the tidal, change direction with every shift of the tide, and these run the fastest of all. Ocean currents run on and on in one direction, determined by wind patterns almost as inexorable, and by the earth's rotation. The sum effect of all the shallow and deep ocean currents is to equalize. Thus, the great Gulf Stream carries warm water north and east through the Atlantic. Then other currents move down the coast of Europe, and west along the Equator, in effect closing the circuit. Most currents move at between one and six knots; even the slowest is strong enough to affect shipping.

Certainly, currents affect the free-swimming skin diver, who soon learns that the best thing to do is get out of them or swim with them. Beating against a current will soon tire the strongest swimmer. If a diver wants to stay in a spot where a current is running, he must cling to a handy wreck, tough sea plant, coral, or rock.

Fish know and accept the value of currents. Often, a diver can see them lazily using a current, drifting along in its sweep. In the Gulf Stream, two divers reported watching a hammerhead shark taking his ease, consuming the food that flowed past him. He didn't bother to pursue tasty baby rays that were just out of reach, but accepted whatever happened to flow into his maw.

One of the strange phenomena born of the currents is the Sargasso Sea, an area of the North Atlantic bounded by the great circling currents. It is a sort of "dead air" space some three million square miles in area, where millions of tons of floating sargassum weed have accumulated over the ages. In legend, the weeds were said to be so thickly tangled as to trap a sailing vessel; they aren't, really. But the Sargasso Sea would probably make a fantastic skin diving site. The weeds, floated by millions of tiny air bladders, are inhabited by billions of living creatures—sea slugs, crabs, shrimp, and tiny one-celled animals. Most of them have become adapted to life on this tangled platform in the open sea, having originally been tidal creatures torn from their normal habitat when wind and waves took their seaweed refuge out to sea.

Temperatures. Currents are one of the factors that affect the temperature of water. Off the northwestern United States, the Alaskan Current and Subarctic Current keep the waters chilled, even in summer, to as low as fifty degrees. Diving here is much more arduous than in southern waters. The same is true of the northeastern coastal seas, chilled by the Labrador and North Atlantic Currents. Underwater swimmers in these areas wear rubber suits to guard against cold.

The temperature of water varies, too, with depth. The sun's rays penetrate only a little way, and of these rays, the warming reds are absorbed within relatively few feet; non-warming ultraviolet rays penetrate to a record six hundred feet but two hundred feet is more common. So as the swimmer goes down, even in tropical waters, the temperature often drops.

Visibility. Visibility also varies with depth, and is, of course, an important consideration in underwater activity. Wind and currents affect visibility, too. Storms and choppy weather, and even a stiff breeze, can cloud the water. Wind makes waves, and waves disturb the shallow bottoms, shifting sand and mud, and churning up the microscopic particles that fill every cubic foot of sea. A swimmer making his way down through the water can enter a sub-surface current carrying such particles. Sometimes, the water at three fathoms (eighteen feet) may be clear, while the four-fathom level is turbid. Then, below this layer of bad visibility, the water may be clear again.

The cloudy layers sometimes contain surprises for skin divers. In the lower archipelago of the Bahamas, two lung divers were suspended about four fathoms down, waiting for a companion who was above them in a turbid layer of water. He finally showed up—sitting astride a loggerhead turtle. He had met the turtle in the cloudy water, as it was coming up for air. It was an unplanned rendezvous, but he was quick to grab the nape of the shell with one hand and the base with the other. The turtle dove, and the diver held on, waved to his surprised friends, and rode down another fifty feet on his underwater sled before releasing his hold. The turtle swam into the deeps.

LIFE UNDERNEATH THE SURFACE

The most overpoweringly constant movement in the sea is not the activity of skin divers, not the flashing of fish, or the drifting of jellyfish, but the steady, slow falling toward the bottom of plant, animal, and inorganic matter. Almost everything that does not decompose eventually reaches the bottom, there to contribute its infinitesimally tiny bit to the sediments that carpet the ocean floor, in many places, thousands of feet deep. This is what Rachel Carson calls "the most stupendous 'snowfall' the earth has ever seen." It is made up of the silt and stones and grains of sand brought into the ocean by the rivers; of lava dust and sand, carried by the wind to sea; and above all, it is made up of the shells and skeletons of sea organisms.

Before the falling "snow" becomes sediment, while it is still largely alive with a primitive sort of life, it is the basis of the sea's natural economy. It all begins with the tiny one-celled plants that float near the surface, nourished by the water's minerals and sustained by the rays of the sun. These, in turn, feed myriad one-celled microscopic animals called protozoa, and even larger creatures like baby crabs, barnacles, and small fish—and the smallest meat-eaters, in turn, live on them. All these creatures together make up what is known as plankton, the mass of life that lives passively in the sea, unable to move except where the currents carry it. Some of it drifts slowly down to lower levels, providing food for deep-living fish.

The ocean has been described as one vast battle-ground, with each class of sea creature preying on smaller ones and, in turn, being preyed upon by larger—or at least more efficient —ones. From the little grunts, which feed on fish eggs, all the way up to the giant sperm whales, which eat the squid they clash with in great battles deep in the abyss, the cycle goes on, with each creature seeking food and fleeing those that consider it their food.

In twenty-five feet of water off the coast of Crooked Island in the Bahamas, I watched the story of fish-eat-fish well dramatized. From a front-row seat on a yellow brain coral I watched sea life at work. A school of cubbyu were feeding on polyps, the tiny invertebrate animals that make coral. Suddenly a small snapper gulped down one of the little wigglers. The cubbyu school scattered into its coral hiding places, with the exception of one, which lagged behind. The snapper was about to devour him too when, just as his mouth closed on the cubbyu, a fast-moving barracuda, about three feet long, whipped into view. In a lightning maneuver, the 'cuda gobbled up both snapper and cubbyu, and swished away, chomping on the two smaller fish.

So the battle goes on. But there seems no likelihood of the sea's being emptied of fish or other creatures. More eggs are deposited than can ever be hatched. A single oyster can produce sixty million eggs a year, a cod eight million. Billions of herring school through the ocean, and each pregnant female lays about fifty thousand eggs a year.

Novice spearfishermen and other divers are amazed when they see the enormous quantities of fish in the sea. Surface anglers can have no idea of the tremendous tonnage of fish that ignore their baited hooks. Some of us have sat on underwater rocks or coral heads, watching the lines of desperate bottom fishermen along the reefs off the coast of Florida. Some anglers use shrimp as bait, some stripped mullet, and others conch meat. Once we counted seventy-two sniffs at bait on one line, during an afternoon about which the fisherman later complained, "Not one nibble." The bloated stomachs of the gray snappers, idling around the anchored boat, told the story: they were stuffed full of polyps from the organ-pipe coral. Not even a live shrimp, a real sea delicacy, would entice them. The anglers wiggled their lines, raised and lowered them—but no snapper did any more than sniff, and only the inquisitive ones did that. None of the seven lines caught anything, and finally the boat churned away, the wake of the propellers looking actually angry. But no one was at fault. The fish just weren't hungry. The anglers were quite right in thinking there were fish under that reef—but what the fish needed more than bait was bicarbonate of soda.

Now, in addition to all the fish, the sea contains men—strange Martian creatures with bulging goggles, air tanks, and great foot-flippers. Perhaps the fish are as puzzled by the men as the men are by the mysteries of the sea.

There is no doubt about it; men are still puzzled. For all the twentieth century's inventions, we have yet to learn much about the ocean and its inhabitants. Better instruments and new techniques will slowly probe into the great depths. But meanwhile at least, the shallows are becoming familiar to more and more humans. The beaches and coves are increasingly populated by inquisitive skin divers. They are, for the most part, an adventurous lot of young people who have, in developing a new sport and pastime, learned how to exist freely and at ease in the water for an hour or so—a feat that only men of vision like Jules Verne would have figured on a century ago.

~~~~~~ *3*

Just Looking

THE FIRST TIME anyone goes under the surface he becomes a looker. Before he announces himself as a spearman, he must first be a looker. He can't spear a fish unless he first seeks it. Because there is so much of interest to see, even the man who has predetermined to practice a specialty immediately upon entering the water becomes fascinated with the lure to look and look.

A NEW VERSION OF BIRD-WATCHING, ELEMENTARY AND ADVANCED

Some underwater enthusiasts never graduate from the looking stage. They are simply satisfied to study life under the sea. It is forever moving; there is no static life. In the calmest seas the rooted plants keep swaying with the underwater cur-

28

rents. Even when fish appear to be suspended motionless in water, they are not completely idle. Let a tasty tidbit flow past them, and they immediately scoop it up. Unless, of course, they're sleeping. Or do fish sleep? Who knows? They have no eyelids, and we have no way of knowing if they are asleep since their eyes are always open. When you spend a lot of time watching fish, you begin to wonder about things like that. You get to feel pretty friendly with fish.

Consider the man I know who has taken to the sport with particular delight. No other pastime pleases him any longer. His investment: a Scott Hydro-Pak, lead weight, flippers, mask, knife, and a policeman's billy to which he's fastened a sharp spike for fending off large fish. He dives down to depths not exceeding sixty feet, selects a rock or coral head, and there he sits. Lately, he's invested in a lead-weighted aluminum and canvas yacht chair. He sits in the chair on the ocean bottom and simply watches life revolve around him. Says he, "The waters belong to the fish. I'm not an intruder—just an observer."

For diversity he once trapped a ten-pound grouper and a half-dozen grunts in a wire fish trap. He placed the fish in separate glass aquariums at several different locations—his home, a downtown cocktail lounge, and occasionally drove the aquariums through the streets on the tail gate of his station wagon. He then returned the fish to the same sea from which they had come.

His experiment was simply explained: He had had the privilege of visiting the fish's world, and he thought he would select a representation of fish to visit our world. The tanks served the purpose. At the cocktail lounge, they were given tidbits of chicken à la king, which they relished; broiled swordfish with *beurre noire* sauce, which they ate hesitatingly; and apple pie, which the grouper gulped down unmannerly. (He broke water several times for second and even third helpings.)

What were the fishes' reactions to their eathly jaunt? Returned to the same reef from which they had come, lowered in the same fish trap and released, they scampered away immediately. The grunts disappeared among the reef, but the grouper poked his head out from his favorite hole and casually—not immediately, but casually—swam over to the friend who had once served him cooked swordfish and apple pie.

From that moment on they were inseparable buddies. The grouper was named Wa-ki, and it was rare that he would stray more than a dozen yards from his earthly companion. Such unusual compatibility and loyalty was unknown. Wa-ki would feed on pieces of conch that his friend would bring along, and often, Wa-ki would put his nose into his buddy's pocket for extra conch. And on days when there was no conch, Wa-ki would nudge his friend and really make the nudge felt.

They became constant hunting companions. The hunter would spear fish, and Wa-ki had them eaten almost before the spear was retrieved. This was a perfect arrangement for the grouper. He had man trained to supply him his daily food— an arrangement that perhaps had never been duplicated before.

Wa-ki was affectionate—a strange sensitivity in fish. Or is it unusual? Wa-ki greeted his friend every day with an affectionate nudge on the arm, would then have his belly scratched, and seemed to enjoy it.

Fish loyalty may never have been exhibited before, but Wa-ki was a one-fish alarm system. A blue shark came nosing down to his friend's idyllic spot one afternoon. Wa-ki came skidding through the legs of the chair as though intending to upset it. He sped away to the coral reef and disappeared into his hole. That was unusual. Wa-ki had never acted that way before. His friend whirled around to find the reason—and saw the blue shark. The shark seemed disinterested and continued swimming into deeper water. Wa-ki came out of hiding and was rewarded with a handful of conch and a long scratching of his belly.

Another friendly grouper was recently discovered on Captain Cousteau's Calypso expedition in the Indian Ocean. Ulysses, a sixty-pound grouper, became a pet of the underwater exploration group. He played with and followed the lung divers during their day's work. He was fed and scratched —two luxuries Ulysses enjoyed that millions of his brethren did not share from earth men. But Ulysses also became a pest at times and had to be jailed in a steel bar anti-shark cage.

The stories of Wa-ki and Ulysses are case histories of advanced fish-watching. Before going as far as entertaining groupers, the looker usually entertains himself with elementary watching. These rare doings of the groupers—easily recognized as one of the more friendly and more inquisitive fish of the seas—clearly establish the fraternization that can result from the meeting of man and fish.

With mask and fins, and sometimes a snorkel, armies of lookers have invaded the waters of all our seacoasts, freshwater lakes through Minnesota, Wisconsin, Nevada, Maine, and Ohio, and most rivers. They are lookers—they only want to see what is in the water. They want to know how the bottom looks, where the fish swim, and how they swim. What do they eat, how do they get their food, what colors are there in the seas, is it dark underwater? A fresh inquisitiveness has come

over a part of the population. The lookers constitute the largest single group among underwater devotees in the country
today. Who are they?

They range from grandparents to children. The lookers
are amateurs, most of whom later become specialists in one
activity of the sport or another. They float on the surface of
the water or merely duck their heads under for a look. They
want to see where they've been before without benefit of the
mask that now opens new horizons. At first they are clumsy,
splashing about wildly, certain to scare the fish in their vicinity. Later they calm down and become more proficient. They
are thrilled at seeing schools of grunts or jacks or grey snappers swim by as casually as though there were no intruders.
They watch the slow-moving conch travel the bottom of
tropical waters, moving his shell home along with every inch
of motion; sea cucumbers that squirt water thrill the children.
Starfish, the real scavengers of the sea, are alive, forever attacking shellfish. All lookers seem to collect them.

This looking is actually a fishy version of bird-watching,
one probably undreamed of by the late John James Audubon,
a most famous naturalist. The habits of most fish have hereto-
fore been studied in glass aquariums, under forced or artificial
conditions. Few ichthyologists in the past have mingled with
fish in their natural environment. Now, scientists are joining
the millions of lookers in bodies of water everywhere, better
to study the habits of fish. Perhaps one will paint and better describe the habits of fish we know, and those which we don't
know, as Audubon painted and studied bird life.

The "lookers" can be divided into three progressive
classes: those who look from the surface with mask and
snorkel, riding the surface waves; those who drift down to

three and five feet, examining coral heads, rocks, kelp beds, eel grass, and the exciting colorful fauna that is ever moved by the underwater currents; and those who graduate to lower levels—twenty and thirty feet and beyond, for the more hearty. By the time they are that far down, they are seasoned skin divers.

WHAT TO SEE AND WHERE TO SEE IT

Where can the looker look and what is he likely to encounter in each of the locales where such looking is done?

The Pacific coastline. On the West Coast, from San Diego south along Baja (Lower) California, the peninsula that affords both ocean as well as leeward observation, the waters are thick with organic matter. Here the looker can watch the daily cannibalism of the seas. The one-celled animals make rich food for the schools of sardines and anchovies that visit the waters in the early morning hours. These, in turn, provide food for the invading deep-water fish, who are eventually scared off by sharks and other predators. Thousands of sea gulls and pelicans also join the foray, plucking tidbits that the larger fish have stampeded.

Rocks abound in these waters, and yellowtail and bass, corbinas, croakers and surf perch can always be found eating marine vegetation around the rocks. Kelp beds are thick along the shores, even extending miles out to sea, providing weird submarine sights for the looker and excitement for the spearman. The kelp roots twine deep into the waters, making complex shadows that sway like giant octopus tentacles. Natural rock breakwaters provide protected underwater gardens whose myriad colored fish and plant life make it almost impossible for the looker to move to another location. He is fascinated with the swaying plumage of the kelp and sea fans, moving with the rhythm of the tides.

Here, too, live the table fish and, outside the kelp beds, roving atop the sunken plateaus and ravines that constitute the underwater mountains several miles off the coastline, are the rugged marlins, mako sharks, and broadbills. Tuna churn up the waters in late spring and early summer. Bluefin tuna come offshore, and the highly prized yellowfin swim up from Mexico waters. Albacore also invade Southern California waters at this time, running from ten to sixty pounds, and occasionally more.

The next stretch to the north is one of the most popular underwater sites in the country for looking and fish spearing —Southern California waters stretching as far south as San Diego and including the prized waters of Santa Catalina Island, southwest of Long Beach.

The shores are rocky, and every type of bottom can be found here: reefs and banks, dunes and sandy bottoms, steep cliffs, caves, shallow and deep waters. The looker can find all that nature has provided underwater. Hundreds of sites have become famous along this, one of the most active underwater areas of the world. The warm Japanese, California, and North Equatorial currents permit swimming the year round, although the summer months are more comfortable. Enthusiasts by the thousands have flocked to the beaches of Laguna, Dana Point, and La Jolla. Many other areas are favorites of natives, as well as thousands of visitors to the California coastline. Catalina Island is almost overrun with divers, many of whom are taken there from the mainland on day excursion boats that rent all the underwater equipment needed. Known spots where fish feed on rocky and kelp bottoms are pointed out by the boat captains who also instruct in the use of equipment.

Three additional islands are included in the area: San Clemente, southwest of Catalina; Santa Barbara Islet; and San Nicholas, which is unprotected and due west of Catalina.

For the looker there are enchanting sunken gardens and tropical fish by the school. The spearsmen will find that hundreds of varieties of fish live in the local waters and other hundreds migrate to and from the coastline. Big-game anglers have for years fished the out-waters of the California coast for such prizes as the bluefin tuna, the broadbill swordfish, and the marlin. The more hearty spearmen have surfaced with giant sea bass and other popular members of the bass family: the black, striped, white, kelp, and rock bass—croakers, abalones, lobsters, sheepshead, barracudas, bonitos, yellowtails, halibuts, skipjacks, and lingcods. Sharks are common along this coastline. But the top spearfishing achievement of them all is spearing a four hundred-pound giant black sea bass among the bottom rocks. These monsters (they sometimes reach six hundred pounds) are favorite rock fishing game even among anglers; the added excitement that attends seeking them out of their underwater lairs has made black sea bass popular game for the mask-and-spear men.

Northward to San Francisco and beyond, the striped bass are favorites, with salmon and trout in hot pursuit. The bass of San Francisco Bay seldom go through Golden Gate since there is an abundance of shrimp to feed upon in the bay. Monterey Bay, south of San Francisco, seems to be a meeting place of the tropical and northern fish. This crossroad often brings salmon face to face with hammerhead sharks or albacore and bonitos and, occasionally, trout.

Northward to Oregon and Washington, where the waters are cold enough for rubber suits, the king of the Pacific coastline is the salmon. The shores are rocky and beautiful, and steelheads, shad, striped bass, halibut, and black rockfish are plentiful. Northern currents keep the waters clear, and vision is fair to good. Plankton, the fish food, is found in large quantities—one reason why there is never a scarcity of fish in these northern waters.

In the Columbia River, Chinook salmon, weighing up to fifty pounds, annually fight the rapids and man-made reservoirs to return to their spawning grounds. Their homing instincts, which return them to their locale of early life, have never been explained satisfactorily, but up the river they swim, after fighting the elements at sea from one to five years.

At Celilo Falls, only the Celilo Indians are permitted to spear salmon from the rivers—a continuation of their old Indian heritage. White men can catch salmon in any other way but with the primitive hand spear.

It is primarily in warmer waters that the popularity of underwater exploration has spread. Mexicans and American tourists have found the West Coast of Mexico ideal for their new sport. Acapulco has become the Mexican capital for the sportsman. The Gulf of Tehuantepec at the southernmost point of Mexico, where it joins with Guatemala and the other Central American republics, teems with activity.

Around the Gulf of Mexico. On the eastern slopes of the Gulf of Mexico, from Yucatan along the shores of Veracruz and Tampico and up to Matamoros, most tropical fish and vegetation can be seen. Natives are anxious to help, and boats and guides are plentiful. Even the Mexican peasants understand the meaning of the underwater sport, and where there is no common language between the natives and visiting foreigners, there is the common bond of their activity. Together, they dive into the clear waters of the Gulf, inspecting the rocky caverns of the Laguna de Terminos and its protecting reef, which rims the Gulf of Campeche. Together, they spear barracudas and groupers, grey snappers and rays.

From Brownsville, Texas, the southernmost city attached to the mainland of the United States, a protecting reef skirts along most of the shoreline of Texas, Louisiana, Mississippi, and Alabama all the way to Carabelle, Florida. But from that point on, all along the western coastline of Florida in the Gulf of Mexico, to the Straits of Florida where the Atlantic Ocean meets with the Gulf, underwater people have been invading the warm waters in droves. Residents along the entire shoreline of Gulf states and visitors to these southern shores come with underwater gear that takes them into the tropical waters.

Most tropical fish can be found in these waters. Rock fish are plentiful. The grouper and its cousins the jewfish are creatures of habit. Timid fish with weak eyesight, they blend in with the contours of the Gulf, making their homes among the rocks and coral. Sea urchins are everywhere, and their spines entering the feet of divers cause more aggravation than predators do.

Bahamian natives use many local remedies against the brittle spines of these urchins. The most popular treatment is to hold the affected part as close to a match or fire as possible, which stops the pain almost immediately. Natives then pry out the spine with a needle and coat the affected part with olive oil.

As in all waters, the rocks and vegetation of the Gulf are

the oases of the sea. Here the native and migrant fish mingle. Edible plant life and small eating fish abound. Sharks and barracudas visit these shallows for their dinner. There is speculation as to when these larger fish can be found among the rocks. They come when they get hungry. We have seen hammerhead and tiger sharks as well as sand and nurse sharks in shallow waters in the early morning hours as frequently as at noon and at dusk. An empty stomach is not dictated to by the time of day.

Lookers here, as in other locales, float on the surface with mask and snorkel and watch the movements of underwater life. In these Gulf waters one finds coral heads, the peacock plumage of the seas. They are every color of the rainbow—white, yellow, and strange mixtures of other colors. The sea fans are purple and yellow and red. Tropical fish of every description and color wiggle in and out of the coral formations that resemble tiny and giant tree branches, antlers of the majestic Scottish stag, embroidery of intricate Alençon lace; mounds of coral brain structure resemble spreading mountain tops.

The Florida Keys. The Florida Keys are truly one of the last frontiers to be discovered and cultivated in the United States. Along the Keys, the Overseas Highway, an extension of U.S. 1, travels from Homestead, Florida, to Key West, the southernmost city of our country, over a watery route. Bridges of concrete, steel, and roadway leap along over interconnected islands that form the roadbed of this amazing auto highway. Until World War II there was no road completing the circuit over the many islands, and no piped drinking water was available to the scattered homesteaders, called "conchs," who lived in this mosquito-infested country.

The waters off shore are shallow and clear. The Gulf Stream flows swiftly just south and east of the entire chain of Keys, carrying with it mud and sediment found in the waters. The stream thus keeps the Florida Keys clear, ideal for underwater exploration. Old-time natives of Key West and U.S. Naval personnel form the bulk of the population of this city, in which Spanish as well as English is spoken on the streets and in business houses. Key Westers took to the water with mask and spear early during the trend to the sport. The natural environment contributed greatly to the early popularity of the sport here.

Fish were plentiful. Islands offered both protected and open waters for every type of underwater devotee. The outside reef protected the archipelago from pounding by waters from the ship channel going to Cuba, and Central and South America. Underwater sites, therefore, were scattered, with both shallow, inshore and deep-water locations.

On one spearfishing expedition to a distant coral reef several miles out from Cudjoe Key, we were examining the base of the reef in some twenty-five feet of water. Upon rounding an extruded coral network, we encountered not the jewfish we were seeking, but another diver—a complete stranger to us. Here, some five miles offshore in open ocean waters, it seemed strange to suddenly come upon another of our own kind instead of a fish. We greeted one another with a friendly wave of the hand no differently than we might wave to one another on the corner of Main and Elm Streets. He smiled and I returned it, both smiles lost amidst the escaping air bubbles of our lungs.

He continued on his way around the reef, and I went on in the opposite direction. But I had not kicked three times

with my flippers when facing me—directly behind the slip-
stream of my new underwater acquaintance—was a barracuda fully three and one half feet long, chomping his jaws
as they always seem to be doing. I let out a yell and jabbed
the open water with my gun. The barracuda retreated and
paid no more attention to us. Later, my friend told me he
was not really keeping company with the 'cuda and had no
idea it was trailing him.

Marathon, the Matecumbe Keys, Tavernier, Key Largo,
and Homestead have become underwater headquarters along
this ocean route. All along the road one can see bobbing heads
of spearmen and lookers on the ocean's surface. Treasure
hunters are also frequently found among the islands, as tales
of buried pirate treasures are constantly heard along the
Highway.

The surface angler is not to be outdone, and along each
of the many bridges that span connecting islands, fishermen
cast their lines for tarpons, groupers, snappers, and barracudas.

Florida lobsters, commonly known as crawfish, are the
delicacies of these waters. They are found in relatively shallow water, and the underwater diver catches them during the
non-spawning season with gloved hands, hand spears, and
twin-tined gigs. One beachcomber, who built his home on one
of the Florida Keys, found a ready-made deep freeze for
lobster. He settled on an island at the perimeter of an excavated hole in the ocean, where a dragline had cleaned out a
blasted area for highway fill. Diving into this excavated hole,
which he used as a swimming pool, he soon discovered that
lobster by the thousands made their home in the broken coral
rock that formed its edges. At dinnertime the beachcomber

would dive into his live stockpile of lobster and bring out enough to feed himself. When guests arrived, he simply brought out enough to make charcoal broiled lobster for everyone.

Miami and vicinity. Miami is the southeastern headquarters for the underwater devotees. Tourists flock to the glass-bottom sight-seeing boats, which dock all along its waterfront. Sunken gardens of tropical luxuriance are everywhere. Underwater fauna, which artists seldom capture, can be seen by millions of tourists who visit the state annually. But for the more aggressive looker there is no substitute for the real thing. Plateaus of rainbow-colored sea fans, pink and rose vestlets, and purple pufflets cover the expanse of ocean bottom. Coral heads, swarming with polyp life, provide food and shelter for millions of tiny tropical fish, every color and shape imaginable. Sergeant majors dart in and out of the plant life. Snappers, grunts, and groupers are around the coral reefs by the score. Wherever a looker turns he'll see tropical growth and tropical underwater life.

The protected waters of Biscayne Bay and its many islands offer additional diversity. Reefs and unprotected waters provide thrills for the big-fish hunter, and the sheltered coves and land-locked harbors attract shell collectors and photographers. Visitors can charter boats for a day's excursion to the nearby islands to look at the bottom, or spear anything from grunts to a three hundred-pound jewfish or a tiger shark. An enterprising skipper of a sixty-three foot catamaran has developed a thriving business in day excursions to various spearfishing locations in near waters. Some of the resort hotels in Miami Beach have arrangements with boat captains to take the hotel guests on one-day, weekend, or longer trips.

Some of the more ardent enthusiasts live in the Miami area. Extended safaris to the West Indies in search of treasures, and deep sea film expeditions most always equip and begin in Miami. The University of Miami classes in underwater biology are conducted in local waters, where the professor and the entire class go under with artificial breathing devices. They study underwater flora and fauna, bring back samples for study and dissection in their labs—and, at the same time, the students learn to love the underwater.

The Bahama Island Group. Out in the Atlantic Ocean, east and southeast of Miami, lie the British colonial islands of the Bahamas, a favorite spot for underwater sportsman and adventurer. The closest island to the mainland is Bimini, headquarters of the Lerner Marine Laboratories, site of one of the world's largest natural aquariums, and meeting place for scientists on world field trips. The thousands of islands that compose the network of the Bahamas provide underwater devotees with activities of every kind—fishing, looking, collecting, scientific study, and even treasure-hunting. Andros Island is the largest and is due southwest of Nassau, capital and seat of the Colonial government, and located on the Island of New Providence. From Great Inagua Island in the south, to Grand Bahama and Great Abaco in the north, this stretch of tropical expanse is enchanting, providing waters that are clearer, and at the same time, more filled with fish and exotic wonder than most any body of water on earth.

Natives are friendly, especially in the out-islands away from the highly commercial tourist attractions of Nassau. Waters are generally shallow throughout the Bahamas, except for channels and occasional deeps. Skin diving anywhere is possible. Coral heads harbor fish and vegetation. The bottoms between coral oases are sandy, with mixed scattered scrub plants, sea cucumbers, conchs, starfish, sea urchins, and rays burrowing into the sand. Here also are sea spiders, lost tiny tropical fish seeking their way back to the protection of coral growth, and occasional groupers darting between coral heads.

Cracks in the ocean floor are hiding places of lobsters, rock fish, and groupers. Moray eels cower in coral holes, waiting to pounce on a passing fish. Morays grow to six feet and larger, and they are a menace to skin divers who put their hands into dark holes while seeking lobsters. Many times, lobsters and moray eels share the same hole. This theory has seemed to have been disproved many times, but on close inspection the dual occupants have been discovered.

Natives of the Bahamas are not generally lovers of the underwater. Few of them, and then only the younger and more progressive, enter the water to spear the fish so often eaten at their table. The natives are expert fishermen but are loyal to their drop line and fish traps.

The rest of the West Indies. All of the West Indies islands are becoming more and more known for their splendid underwater sites and spearfishing. In Cuba, and in Jamaica, another of the British colonies, more and more swimmers are going underwater. Haiti has an underwater school at Port-au-Prince, and the Dominican Republic and Puerto Rico likewise have devoted followers. The American-owned Virgin Islands are havens for the sport, and keen interest has been reported all along the Leeward and Windward Islands as far south as Trinidad. All these islands offer the same underwater beauty as the Bahamas and Florida. Shallow waters provide interest and sport for the beginner as well as for the professional underwaterman.

The British island of Bermuda, off the coast of North Carolina, is another ideally situated base. The island is surrounded by several barrier reefs, which protect the land from pounding breakers. The reefs are within sight of one another in relatively shallow waters, making them ideal for sightseeing and spearfishing underwater. Tourists have taken more and more to the mask and fins in these tropical waters during the summer months. Local residents, when not sailing, are diving beneath the waves. One hearty Britisher took her eighteen-month baby underwater with her in a swimming pool. Her child liked dunking so well that she had a mask fashioned for her daughter and, before the child had a complete set of teeth, she was an accomplished underwater swimmer.

From Florida to Maine along the Eastern coastline. Back on the United States mainland, from Miami to Jacksonville, there is avid interest in all forms of diving. Bottoms here are similar to those of southern Florida. But north of Georgia the bottoms lose the romantic coral growth, which is replaced gradually by rocks in more murky waters.

Yet the entire eastern coastline harbors many underwater clubs and scattered, interested individuals, although the waters are too cold for skin diving except during the summer. In mid-winter divers wear dry rubber suits with heavy woolen underwear. They dive into the frigid Atlantic, and into frozen lakes and rivers where holes have been chopped out of the ice.

Fairfield County residents of Connecticut have the Long Island Sound shoreline from Greenwich to Fairfield in which to indulge their sport. The local tabloid-size supplement, *Fairfield County Fair*, reports active spearfishing in Greenwich at Woolsey Rock; in Stamford, Todd Rock is a favorite site, as are Breakwater and Cove Rocks. Other areas are Long Neck Point in Noroton; Fish Island off Tokeneke in Darien; Sprite Island off Norwalk; Cedar Point and Bishops Rock at Westport; Frost Point at Greens Farms; and the Penfield Lighthouse areas in the town of Fairfield. Visibility in these northern waters ranges from fair to poor, depending upon wind and weather. During the summer months, when activity is heaviest, residents and the summer colony of ex-urbanites on both the Connecticut and Long Island shores engage busily in underwater watching, photography, and spearfishing. The northern coastline has less rock than the more interesting south shore, which also shelters more striped and black bass.

During the latter summer months the Gulf Stream brings to the windward shores of Long Island tropical fish, such as the sting ray and hammerhead shark. Occasional wrecks off Montauk Point, Block Island, and Fishers Island, as well as scattered others, make underwater watching interesting for those who venture out to near deep water. But most of the time, Long Island Sound waters are murky as compared with the clear tropical waters of Florida and the Caribbean. All along the mid-Atlantic coast, mud and grass bottoms do not provide the interesting array of sights experienced by the southern native and tourist. But no matter. A New Yorker never before interested in marine life suddenly dives in waters off Montauk Point and becomes fascinated with orange-red gulfweed, eelgrass, and kelp plants. The Long Islander can explore such accessible waters as those of Atlantic Beach and see the wonder of orange sponges that provide food for tiny fish, sea cucumbers that squirt harmless fluids, and crabs making their way along the bottom. Striped bass, moving along their way, suddenly become a living aquarium for the New Jerseyite near Cape May.

In Maine, even in summertime, the water, fed in part by the North Atlantic and Labrador Currents, is usually too cold for skin diving for long periods of time. Rubber suits are commonly used during the summer months.

Fresh water enthusiasts. Among the most popular fresh-water sites for diving in the country are the Great Lakes. The network of Lakes Superior, Huron, Michigan, Erie, and Ontario have brought forth a crop of rugged skin divers who, while they miss the tropical growths and variety of fish of their southern contemporaries, are making their own enthusiastic contribution to the sport. The streams from Canada that feed the Great Lakes bring temperatures lower—especially in waters twenty-five feet and deeper—than in most coastal regions. The deep currents stir up the waters and the bottoms, making visibility more uncertain than in clear oceans. But spearmen in these waters can seek the walleye; muskellunge, the barracuda of the lakes; small-mouth bass; northern pike; yellow perch; and lake herring.

Lake Michigan, especially the southernmost part of the lake, is heavily polluted, and its sandy bottom and sparse vegetation make underwater activity dull. But Great Lakes anglers take more than twenty million pounds of fish annually from its waters, the greater amounts in whitefish, trout, herring, smelt, and pike.

More than eleven thousand lakes dot Michigan alone, many of which are used by divers. The activity in this fresh water area is far greater than most imagine. Wisconsin boasts eight thousand lakes, and Minnesota has more than eleven thousand where fishermen of all sorts try their luck.

Brophy Lake, near Detroit, is the private sanctuary of Ford Motor Company employees and the Ford Seahorses, a group of some twenty-eight underwater devotees. When the Seahorses are not diving in their lake, they meet regularly at the Ford swimming pool where they get and give instruction in diving and safety.

Ice diving has become popular in these northern sectors. Club members and individuals have originated a new winter sport by chopping holes in the ice, through which divers with well-padded rubber suits and lungs have descended into the icy waters with spearguns and life-lines tied to their waists. Northern pike, panfish, and an occasional muskie are speared.

Whether in an ice-hole in Minnesota, or over a reef in the Caribbean, the unusual always seems to happen. It did in Bahamian waters one rainy day. To a diver underneath the surface, rain up above looks something like a school of mullet churning the water. It's exciting to see the rains pour down, unable to touch you because you're under thousands of accumulated gallons of old rain. It also excites the fish. During this particular downpour a small snapper became so excited that it darted wildly to and fro. It must have been in a frenzy when it streaked forth and bit the tail of a motionless barracuda—then, realizing its mistake, it scampered into the nearest protective reef.

CHILDREN LOVE THE SPORT

Probably the largest group of lookers are children. Watching a group of children at the seashore, especially those attempting underwater looking for the first time, is sometimes more amusing than watching clowns.

"Mommy," they shout, running out of the surf, "I saw a fish. A real live fish. It swam right past my nose." And away they run into the surf again before you can comment.

Children to about the age of six sit in the surf with mask firmly attached, ducking under a wave occasionally, screaming, after the wave has passed, that fish of all sorts, sizes, and shapes have passed them. Most of the time it's washed-up seaweed. But seaweed or a floating beer can—the youngsters and their wild imaginations see fish.

Children's equipment need not exceed mask and flippers for the time they spend in the water will be relatively short. They will pummel the waters with arms and legs until taught correctly. But they will be the most amazed at seeing live fish swim under them—especially when the little grunts, the mayfish, gudgeons, and the killifishes swim up to the mask or under their arms. Children have a natural curiosity about many things that interest them, and certainly, communing with the fish takes a foremost interest.

Some children are natural-born swimmers. Those who are fortunate enough to live near the ocean are naturally drawn to the sea from childhood. One such couple of Britons in the Bahamas live, with their family of eight children, not twenty yards from the sea. The windward side of their island home faces the sea; the children used the beach and rocks for their first play yard.

The eldest, at six, was first introduced to spearfishing by an older neighbor of ten. Together, the boys learned their craft with home-styled spears made of beach umbrella rods, pieces of bamboo, strips of rubber made from inner tubes, and a mask. They couldn't afford fins. With the barest of equipment, these novices swam to the rocks a hundred yards off shore; the first day out they speared lobsters and groupers and rock fish. The take fed both their families.

As the younger boy grew older and his brothers became six—that was apparently the family age for spearfishing consent—they fished the waters surrounding their home and the deeper holes farther out in the ocean. They fished for sustenance and supplied fish to their many relatives in Nassau. At fourteen, the eldest, with eight years of experience, could well be an instructor in any underwater spearfishing school.

From these young experts I learned not to barb a spear. It was simple reasoning. If you barb the shaft and spear a fish, the fish will swim off with the spear (if not hit in a vulnerable spot). You then lose both fish and spear. If the spear is unbarbed and you spear a fish poorly, the fish shakes out the spear, leaving it on the ocean floor. You swim after the spear, locate the wounded fish for a second shot, and thus you have both fish and spear instead of neither. The reasoning worked; I watched.

Usually, to be sure, these kids don't give a fish an opportunity to shake out a spear. It's normally lodged in the gills, through the eyes, and into the brain on the first shot. With their simple home-made slings, they once brought home a forty-two pound rock fish.

Four of the younger children—all under ten—were returning from the same rocks one hundred yards offshore one day in 1951. One of the boys had a bleeding grouper on the end of his spear. They were in ten feet of water, heading for shore, when all four sensed and felt a tremendous body dart swiftly among them. It all happened too quickly to re-establish the entire scene, but the grouper was missing from the spear point, and one of the boys was bleeding badly from a head laceration. He was taken ashore and to the hospital for several stitches. Later, the boys decided that a white shark, the deadly species known as the great man-eater, had attacked the group, grazing the head of one of the youths, in an effort to get the bleeding grouper. It was unusual for this shark, which grows to forty feet, to be in such shallow waters.

The boys took a rather light view of the man-eater; they were back in the ocean again the next day.

FISH-WATCHING LEADS TO OTHER SPECIALTIES

Why watch fish? Mostly because it's fun, but there are other reasons, too. The American Indian speared trout in swift-running streams for sustenance. He must have watched fish in order to know their habits so that he could spear them on the run—much as a hunter bags ducks on the wing.

Seine fishermen must know the habits of sardines and herring and shrimp, for without that knowledge of their habits, they would come home with empty nets.

There are serious-minded watchers, too, ichthyologists who, in the interest of science, learn how the fish spends his day. A biologist could watch the female seahorse transfer her eggs to the male for fertilizing, or could watch the really big sharks in the Gulf Stream attack and protect one another. In these warm, moving waters, the great undersea battles take place. Or, in more shallow waters, it's interesting to see how a blunt-nosed nurse shark tears into a sting ray under a coral ledge. Even sharks have their delicacies, and the rays are the apple pie and ice cream of their diet. This underwater battle is fought every minute of the day and night in waters the world over. It is perhaps even more interesting to be right on the sidelines watching the patterns of underwater life than to be a part of the battles. Some people think so, and more and more are devoting their leisure time to fish-watching.

How do they go about it?

The more daring watchers believe they must actually enter the sea, sharing it with the fish they want to see. For them, mask and fins are basic equipment. Some wear artificial breathing devices, and some simply extend a snorkel above the water. Many do it an easier way. They devise their own floating units from which to observe life below. Truck inner tubes are popular on all seaboards, and government surplus one-man rafts serve the same purpose, with more space for moving about. A new fish-watching raft recently came on the market which supports one floater. It has a hole at the bow through which the looker peers, wearing a mask. In this aquatic comfort, with a snorkel for breathing and fins to propel himself, a looker can float all day long without tiring.

The traditional glass-bottom bucket, usually a waterproofed butter tub with a plate glass bottom, has served turtle and bottom fishermen almost since fishing began. A notable offshoot of the bucket is the glass-bottom boat, which acts as a sort of multiple underwater mask for crowds of sightseers, and provides really striking views. One Midwestern garden club lady was so amazed at the beauty of the underwater gardens of Bermuda that she made an excellent collection of 35 mm color slides through the bottom of the boat and is now lecturing on underwater life to clubs in her home town area.

Whether at first hand or from a boat, the earnest watcher

develops a certain admiration for the way fish live. Of course, they do eat one another. How else could they survive? But this eating one another does not go on all the time. When fish are not seeking food, even the most dangerous are at peace with the world, and that's how skin divers are able to get close enough to watch their habits. If they attacked everything strange that entered the sea, the sea would not be as safe as it is. In a peaceful sea the fish are peaceful too. On occasions, tropical reefs have been seen to harbor an indefinite variety of fish, many of them mutual enemies of the worst sort. Barracudas mingle freely with grey snappers and grunts—both tasty tidbits for the big fellows. Nurse sharks lie under a coral ledge enjoying the quiet afternoon, while sting rays burrow into the sand not a dozen feet away.

Lookers are fascinated with sea anemones nestled among the coral growths. They are vivid and colorful. One can't help but notice the eloactis mazelli—it resembles a table decoration—an oversized pink pear with trailing multi-colored fingers stemming from the top. The closed pimplet really looks like the deerstalkers hat of Sherlock Holmes, green with yellow dots. Most of the anemones, and there are hundreds of varieties, have their growth coming to the top, trailing their budding tentacles in the undersea currents. In the North Atlantic, the ringed deeplet resembles an inverted skullcap, crowned with orange and white oversized dewdrops. Anemones, flowerlike in appearance, are really simple living animals. They have a respiration system which permits entry of oxygen from the waters and a digestive system that swallows tidbits from the sea. Offer an anemone a slice of pickled tongue and it will soon disappear. Try a small stone or a piece of wood and it will be rejected.

Corals of the tropics by far are the more beautiful of underwater scenes. Coral is alive, with a skeleton that permits growth to enormous heights. The largest known coral formation is the famous Great Barrier Reef, bounding the east coast of Australia for more than 1250 miles, some ten to ninety miles off shore.

Coral, underwater, resembles gentle swaying fans, or takes the form of an enlarged head, covered with furrows of intricate passages of brain, known as the brain coral. Stag and elk horn coral, too, resemble their nomenclature. Some coral growths are valuable—especially the pinks and reds whose internal skeletons are harder than most. Some must be avoided —the stinging coral produce a sting that pains for days. But when coral is brought to the surface, the living polyps die, taking with them the vivid colors only an underwater diver is privileged to see.

Coral grows in tropical waters whose temperature remains above sixty-eight degrees. Therefore, the coast of the Atlantic seaboard, with the exception of Florida, has no coral formations.

Anglers sometimes become fish-watchers, but few of them will admit it. Most prefer to remain completely ignorant of anything underwater, including such questions of self-interest as what makes fish bite into bait. If all anglers took up underwater fish-watching, chances are, the twenty-five million of them would enjoy their sport more when they returned to it—if they returned to it at all. One can't help but learn the feeding habits of fish by watching them in action. In one case, for example, snappers near a reef in Florida pounced on live shrimp bait as quickly as the bottom fishermen heaved over their lines. On another reef, not three miles from the first, another school of red snappers couldn't have been less interested in live shrimp. Why? The same fish, the same bait, but two different locales. Could it be that a patient fish-watcher could have solved this problem?

Fish-watching has a way of leading to something else, from photography or spearfishing all the way to new businesses.

Two Washington, D.C., men—one of whom got his start underwater while serving with the U.S. Marine Corps in the South Pacific during World War II—recently began a thriving business collecting and selling the timid seahorse. With breathing lungs, masks, and nylon nets, they search along the Maryland shores for these delicate six-inch fish that look like rearing thoroughbreds. In the living rooms of their homes they keep the seahorses, feeding them microscopic shrimp raised in a bowl of salt water. Orders for these sea animals pour into Washington from all parts of the country.

How to Exist and Swim Underwater

IT SEEMS LIKE AN UNFAIR MISTAKE that man can't breathe underwater. After all, water consists of less than 12 per cent hydrogen by weight and more than 88 per cent oxygen. But all that underwater oxygen is quite useless for human breathing; it can't be pulled away from the hydrogen. The oxygen fish extract from water is free oxygen dissolved in it—and it takes gills to get even the free oxygen out of water. Men have lungs instead of gills; lungs work fine on air, and perhaps we should be glad of that.

But man has recently mastered prolonged existence underwater. It came in several stages. The first stage came when a glass faceplate was inserted into a piece of rubber and placed around the eyes and nose, forming a rubber face mask. This mask has revolutionized underwater activity for with it, man has, for two decades or more, really "discovered" the under-seas for the first time. But this basic mask and its supplement, a breathing tube, limit the user to short forays underwater; the skin diver must hold his breath.

That only works for a while, for every tissue of the body requires oxygen to stay alive and do its job. We think of the agony of lungs at a bursting point as being the reason we must surface and breathe again. Actually, the pain is a sort of danger signal, warning us to get rid of the carbon dioxide building up in our lungs and pull in some fresh air laden with oxygen.

The average skin diver can remain below the surface about fifteen to twenty seconds, while the skin diver descending for the first time is excited with even a three-second dunking. The advanced diver remains a full minute, and the diver who has taken the patience to learn deep pre-breathing before descending can remain for two minutes and more.

The invention of artificial breathing devices was the second stage. These enabled divers to breathe compressed air or pure oxygen from steel tanks carried on their backs. The length of time spent underwater now depends upon the volume of air or oxygen that can be crammed into a tank and how it is breathed. This "packaged" breathing permits divers freedom never before experienced with other devices for working or playing below the water's surface.

PRESSURE PUTS ON "THE SQUEEZE"

Swimmers who have never worn any underwater equipment or summer vacationists who swim at the seashore normally have no idea what happens to their bodies when they dive into even ten feet of water. What does happen to a diver's body when he plunges from a six-foot diving board? What does water do to the body?

Before learning what water does, it's advisable to know the atmospheric effect on the body above water. At sea level, 14.7 pounds per square inch (p.s.i.) of pressure bear against the body, or "one atmosphere" of pressure. This is because air has weight and all weight—be it of solid or liquid or a gas like air—exerts some force against a body. At sea level this force against our bodies is not felt; the pressure is equalized by air within our lungs and tissues. The higher we ascend into mountainous areas, the less force there is against our bodies because the air gradually thins out.

But if we descend into only thirty-three feet of water, the pressure against our bodies increases 100 per cent, to 29.4 p.s.i., or two atmospheres. Each foot below sea level increases the pressure 0.445 p.s.i. That means simply this: Each time a diver descends one foot into water, an increase of force of almost half a pound pushes like hundreds of strong thumbs against each square inch of body surface. If a diver were to descend into really deep waters, he would flatten out like a pancake. As an example, going down one mile into the water multiplies the surface pressure by 160, so that more than a ton of constant pressure is exerted against every square inch of body surface. No one can survive at such excruciating pressures. And that's why man has not descended to such depths, except within a steel chamber.

How then does the body react to water?

The body temperature is 98.6 degrees. Heat or chill it a few degrees either way and the body is uncomfortable. Underwater, the same thing is true. Unless the body is accustomed to swimming in fifty-degree water, it will rebel—you feel cold, but bad. Rubber suits have been developed to help the swimmer retain his body heat during cold-water diving.

Underwater pressure is an important lesson for all divers to learn for various parts of the body are affected differently by the pressures of diving. The ears and sinuses will hurt severely if the diver cannot equalize to increased pressures in descending. A light snort normally clears the eustachian tube unless mucus or swelling has stopped the air passage. A skin diver suffering from a cold or affected with sinus trouble is wise to stay out of the water until the ailment clears up.

Too, lung divers who insist on working in waters beyond one hundred feet will feel the effect of nitrogen narcosis, an exhilarated state that comes from breathing nitrogen under extreme pressure. The body pressure is 58.8 p.s.i. at one hundred feet, or four atmospheres. An experienced diver can feel the hopped-up effects of the nitrogen but can safely descend somewhat deeper if he stops all heavy activity. The U.S. Navy advises that narcosis can begin at 125 feet—becoming dangerous at 175 feet. The Navy also considers 250 feet the maximum safe depth for lung divers.

Narcosis has been experienced by many depth divers. It is best described as a blissful state of drunkeness. It weakens or eliminates all coordination and even the basic drive of self-preservation. The degree of narcosis and the depth at which it hits depends upon the diver's stamina and state of mind. Many lives have been lost in deep-dive attempts. When excessive nitrogen begins to dull the senses, the smartest thing is to ascend slowly. Some divers have used a lighter gas like helium mixed with pure oxygen to avoid narcosis. It has proven satisfactory, but it is not recommended to the inexperienced diver.

When using a full face mask with air line attached to a surface compressor, care must be exerted to avoid "face squeeze." Unequal pressure is the cause of this accident, the result of mechanical failure on the part of the air compressor supplying air to the diver. Or a hose clamp could easily become loose—it did in the case of a reasearch diver in the Abaco group of islands in the Bahamas. The clamp gave, dropping the air hose into the water. The scientist was, fortunately, in shallow water, but the sudden lack of air made his eyes start to pop out, and he required immediate medical care.

LEARN TO BREATHE

Another lung-diving body reaction is air embolism. This affects the lungs, the blood stream, and the heart. Air embolism results from undue expansion of the lungs when a diver ascends while holding his breath. The expanding air can rupture the blood vessels and air sacs in the lungs, which results in air bubbles entering the blood system. If a decompression chamber is handy, fast treatment in it is desirable. Divers have risen successfully even from extreme depths after discarding artificial breathing devices. The remaining air in the lungs continues to expand in the rise, since pressures diminish, so a gradual ascent is possible while slowly exhaling.

These reactions, and others, result when the body is subjected to undue pressure or changes in pressure. The body has its own ways of showing dissatisfaction with the abnormal. The best defense against these accidents and underwater diseases is prevention. The one certain method for prevention is complete knowledge and understanding of what taxing pressures do to the body.

GOING DOWN FOR RECORDS, WITH AND WITHOUT ARTIFICIAL BREATHING DEVICES

Captain J. Y. Cousteau, the man who led the French group that developed the presently popular Aqua-Lung, has perhaps contributed more to skin and lung diving than any other single person. His pioneering efforts produced the artificial lung that is, today, theoretically capable of taking a diver down to almost 450 feet, a depth unheard of not more than twelve years ago. No man has yet lived at that depth, not, it is believed, because of the imperfection of the breathing device, but because of nitrogen narcosis.

Narcosis has taken the lives of at least two qualified divers who attempted to learn more about the feeling, and who at the same time tried to establish deep diving records.

Frenchman Maurice Fargues, companion of Cousteau and associates and diving master of the Cousteau diving ship "Elie Monnier," descended to 396 feet and signaled, "Tout va bien" (all is well), according to Cousteau in *The Silent World*. This was the deepest an Aqua-Lung diver had ever descended, but narcosis finally affected Fargues, and he drowned.

Another hopeful, Miami attorney Hope Root, wanted to shatter Frenchman Frederic Dumas' record of 307 feet. A University of Miami oceanographer was on hand to record his descent with a depth-sounder. Root hoped to sign his name on a marker placed at 450 feet. According to sounding reports, he paused at the 445-foot marker. Then, apparently under the effect of narcosis, he went on. The sounding device lost him at 660 feet.

In October, 1954, a Californian, John Clark-Samazon, successfully descended to 350 feet to establish a new lung-diving record. He wore a protective rubber suit and carried three steel tanks containing a mixture of helium and oxygen instead of compressed air.

A woman diver reached 209 feet in 1955 with an artificial breathing device. The woman, Rosalia (Zale) Parry of Santa Monica, California, had been diving a relatively short time. She was taught by Parry Bivens, an aeronautical engineer and a deep-water diver, who descended with her on her record dive. He taught her through long and trying practice dives in swimming pools and later in a homemade pressure chamber built in the backyard of his home. She plans to descend deeper in the near future and hopes, eventually, to beat the gay and zany feeling of narcosis.

Another kind of dive entirely is the common skin dive—still the most popular type of diving—done without artificial breathing devices. The diver descends on free air, and when that air is exhausted, he returns for another lungful. But actually there is little air in the lungs of the deep free-air diver. He breathes deeply, getting air into tissues seldom used. This "pre-breathing" goes on for several minutes, almost exhausting the diver. Try breathing deeply for a minute, and a dizzy feeling and heavy head will result. Deep divers practice this deep breathing, the best way to get volumes of air into the system.

Word came from the Italian Sport Fishing Federation in 1952, recording a 128 foot free-air dive by air force Lieutenant Raimondo Bucher. He went down in the Mediterranean with 8.8 pounds of weight and brought up the marker from that depth to establish what was the diving record of the day. Unofficially, that depth had been penetrated before by natives in the far-flung Pacific and by amateurs elsewhere who had not bothered to get officials to record their descents.

Polynesian divers descend with stone or metal weights at their waists and go down regularly 120 to 165 feet. Pearl and sponge divers of the South Seas, many of them Japanese, often reach the same depth in their daily chores. But these people are earning their livelihood by diving and have practiced their trade since childhood. They are not thinking of records. Greek divers, some of the better men of the underwater, with years of sponge collecting experience, have been known to dive to Bucher's depth, and then some, with regularity.

Feats of this sort are not common, mind you, nor can every man equip himself to descend four atmospheres or more into the water. And it's not recommended for the average weekend diver. In other parts of the world, skin divers can go down 120 feet and more in seeking a diving record. But in Okinawa, native divers consider it a daily chore to spear and net fish at these depths. It's called an Okinawa Fish Drive-in.

This unique method of catching fish involves up to one hundred natives who have been driving-in fish since they could swim, as had their forefathers before them. After deep prebreathing, the heartiest natives take the nets down to 120 feet and set up walls of net about fifty feet high. Nets face one another about fifty feet apart. They terminate in another net compartment into which the fish are herded.

The herding is the unique part. All eligible natives get

into the water about a mile from the net compartment and begin making weird underwater noises by rattling metals and striking rocks together. The noises startle and drive the fish ahead. Natives tread water and move forward, pushing the panicky fish before them. At a point fifty yards from the net-bag, other deep-water divers don small homemade goggles and dive down 120 feet to spear the larger fish who normally offer resistance, thus panicking the smaller ones and driving them into the trap. According to George M. Taggart, U.S. Civil Administrator at the Ryukyus, and one of the renowned fish authorities of the Pacific, "The swimmers dive to 120 feet several times before the drive is over." The less exhausted divers go down to 120 feet for the last time to tie the net ends together, forming an immense bag in which the fish are captive. The bag is hand hauled to the surface and the fish are distributed to everyone in the village.

Okinawan natives, as a heritage, have been deep diving for generations, and little has been thought of the feat. At times, Polynesians, according to known authorities, dive deeper than 120 feet since they are said to be the most accomplished pearl divers in the world, closely rivaled by the Japanese.

Underwater activity, from spearfishing to shell collecting, is exhausting. Suppressed movement against pressures greater than the earth's atmosphere will burn up energy faster than any land activity. Diving beats weight lifting, wrestling, or tennis. In fact, it is the fastest known method for reducing. An underwater adventurer we know sought sunken treasures for two weeks, diving from six to ten hours daily. He weighed in thirty-two and one-half pounds lighter.

Or consider the method of reducing established by one

overweight couple. They packed a box of calorie charts, diets, girdles, therapeutic prescriptions, weights, pills, and medical advice, took it with them to the bottom of Long Island Sound, and there abandoned it. At the end of an active summer of spearfishing and shell collecting, together they tipped the scales fifty-seven pounds lighter.

SAFETY PRECAUTIONS CAN PREVENT ACCIDENTS

In shutting out a known world for an unknown, a certain element of fear naturally arises. That's okay. Fear brings healthier respect for underwater safety, a point that can never be overstressed.

Learning to relax in this strange new element is one of the biggest jobs an underwater devotee can undertake. It's only natural to be constantly on the lookout for a lurking barracuda or a crouched moray eel in his hole. Like an alert pilot in war, the underwater diver is forever surveying the waters ahead and above—with not infrequent checks to the rear.

One rule worth remembering is that salt water and air work for the swimmer; he should try not to fight them. Swimming in salt water, an unburdened man has positive buoyancy. The air in his lungs will enable him to remain afloat on the surface—if he relaxes. If he fights the water— and himself—he'll probably panic. Therefore, *relax*. You are buoyant with only a lungful of air, and with replenishment of that lungful of air, you can float on the water for days—if necessary—if involved in an air or boat accident.

Not only is it important to relax on the surface—but likewise underwater. Whether freediving, with no artificial breathing devices, or lungdiving, with self-contained breathing devices, it is still important to retain complete composure. Being in an abnormal environment requires abnormal use of senses. Therefore, there should be absolute coordination of the body, sight, brain, and physical ability. The mind should be razor-keen to be able to pass along instantaneous corrective measures for undue ear pressure, or to warn a lung diver why he should not enter a narrow cave entrance or a blocked passageway in a wecked ship. Coordination of sight and physical prowess is necessary for keeping out of the tangle of kelp and eel grass, and other underwater obstacles.

The idea of underwater activity is exciting, and each of its branches commands the time and interests of its devotees. That's all very well, but underwater diving is supposed to be temporary. We must return to the surface eventually.

All underwater enthusiasts should enjoy good health. The activity is taxing, and a physically sound body is necessary to keep up with a diver who insists on chasing a fish along the ocean bottom into his lair. Divers who are overweight, who suffer from respiratory or nervous disorders, ear or sinus trouble, those who easily suffer from air or sea sickness or claustrophobia, and those who have heart conditions should not enter the underwater.

Those who pass the Red Cross surface swimming tests are candidates for the more hazardous underwater tests, which could include self-checkouts. One might try these for example: Dive to twenty feet without feeling ear pain; remove water from a mask while underwater; swim underwater for at least fifty feet without the use of fins or breathing devices; bring up a disabled diver lying helplessly in tangled kelp— or rescue a diver from a minimum of fifteen feet; master the treacherous rip tide; learn to ditch equipment, like lead belts or breathing devices, and to cut loose from the tangled lines of a speargun.

These primary safety measures will qualify anyone for extended underwater activity. The important thing, under conditions of duress, is to keep your head. A diver in panic will not only endanger his own life but will drag his companions into trouble.

Trouble with fish is far in the minority when compared with other underwater accidents. Accidents come as a result of panic and lack of understanding of underwater pressure. When using artificial lungs, a diver who suddenly uses up his air supply and finds himself in sixty feet of water or more has himself to blame. All recommended commercial equipment comes with a reserve air supply that will at least enable a diver to surface when the air in his main tank runs out. If the diver elects to remain below, after he's switched to his reserve supply—he's asking for trouble.

Divers have also been known to panic in shallow water. The mere envelopment of water causes many divers to feel lost. If this feeling continues, the best advice is to find another sport.

THE PRIMARY DANGERS

Underwater accidents are common. One of the most common is the inability to equalize the body to the increased pressure as one descends into deeper water. The ears and sinus are most immediately affected. The head feels swelled, as when quickly rising or descending in an airplane. Pain in the ears results from swelling of the eustachian tube, a bony tube that connects the middle ear with the nasopharynx and equalizes air pressure on both sides of the tympanic membrane (ear drum). If a diver is a sinus sufferer, he has no business in the water. Pressure will also cause mucus to block the sinus passages, which, in turn, causes pain.

Normally, ear pain can be eliminated by swallowing, or by rising a few feet to a level of lesser pressure. Another method is to clear the passages from the middle ear to the throat by pressing the nose against the face plate of the mask and blowing smartly. Continued diving will soon teach the diver to equalize to the pressure of lower depths.

The squeeze. Depth produces increased pressures, and if sufficient air is not present in the cells and tissues to equalize the outer pressures, a body or face "squeeze" results. Sometimes the eyes pop out. The chest walls can cave in like a coal mine whose supporting beams have been removed. A diver can easily die without knowing what hit him.

How does the squeeze work? If the air compressor supplying air to a hose diver suddenly stops while the diver is as deep as forty or sixty feet, and the diver is working without a reserve emergency air tank, his face can "squeeze" into a shapeless mass.

How does one prevent the face squeeze? Have a knowledgeable man tending the compressor and another man handling the lines. Double check all hose couplings and keep the gas tank full. A safety valve at the mask and an automatic switch-over tank can also prevent such disasters.

In skin diving, especially by those who seek depth records, the volume of air a diver takes down with him in his lungs automatically compresses, at a ratio of about four to one at one hundred feet. When the diver reaches his saturation point, or that point of his dive where he is unable to feel comfortable due to exhaling restriction, he had better surface. Enroute to the surface, the outside pressure on his body lessens, and the remaining air in his lungs and tissues expands. If, however, the diver elects to go deeper than his saturation point, he'll never know why.

One thing no diver should do is to continue diving when there is pain and pressure at the ears. The pain will not ease the deeper one goes. It gets worse, since pressure increases at a rate of .0445 per foot. Pressure against the ear drums causes the pain. Eventually, the ear drum will puncture, and a hemorrhage will result.

Air embolism. In relatively shallow water a diver can easily rupture the lungs. The first rule to learn—whether diving with or without breathing devices—is *do not hold your breath in rising from any depth*. I want to repeat this rule throughout elementary, as well as advanced, instruction. It will save your life. You cannot beat the physics of the body, so learn to live with it.

Air embolism is simply more air within the lungs than the lungs can handle. How can you have too much air in the lungs? Easily! In rising, the pressure lessens and automatically expands the air in the lungs to greater volume. To what volume depends upon the depth at the beginning of the ascent. If the diver is not expelling the expanding air, the blood vessels in the lung will rupture. Air must have an outlet, too. Air bubbles move swiftly, as the escaping air bubbles of captured carbonated drinks when the cap is removed. The same thing happens in the lungs. Excess air must go somewhere, and since the blood vessels of the lung are ruptured, the bubbles flow into the blood stream and thus into the heart and the arteries.

Affected are the chest, brain, limbs, and heart. Death can result—and it's so unnecessary. If divers will learn to breathe normally under all circumstances and expel air gradually in ascending—whether the conditions are normal or emergent—they will survive.

Learn to recognize air embolism in a companion: loss of consciousness, dizziness, convulsions, froth at the mouth, severe chest pain, partial paralysis of the limbs. A diver may surface with these symptoms. Treatment: Get the victim to a pressure chamber as quickly as possible and step up the pressure six atmospheres so that the excess air bubbles in the blood stream will disappear. Then decompress to normal pressure.

Decompression is the gradual return from abnormal pressures back to atmospheric pressure. This lifesaving method, returning the body to normal atmospheric pressure of 14.7 p.s.i. after a deep dive, can be done in either of two ways. The routine method is to return gradually to the surface, in accordance with the published U.S. Navy Decompression Tables, which stipulate the number of pauses and the duration of each pause at varying levels, depending upon the depth of the dive. The second method of decompression, ordinarily used only after a rapid decompression accident, is in a decompression chamber that can be filled with air under pressure simulating that at which the diver has been, and gradually brings the body back to atmospheric pressure at sea level.

Bends. A diver is subject to the "bends," or the caisson disease. This is induced by rising too rapidly, causing too rapid a decrease in air pressure after a prolonged stay in a deep compressed atmosphere. What happens is that at high pressures, an overabundance of nitrogen (about 78% of air is nitrogen) goes into solution in the blood system and tissues. At reduced pressure (pressures reduce as we rise in the water), the nitrogen bubbles come out of solution in the blood. These bubbles of gas travel through the blood stream. They can lodge in the heart and cause instant death, or may travel to the brain or to the spinal cord and cause various forms of paralysis.

Divers are affected with caisson disease in varying degrees. Overweight, overindulgence in alcohol, and a generally rundown condition will all tend toward the disease, which affects younger and more hearty divers less than older men who are badly out of condition.

Recognizable symptoms of the bends are inability to use limbs, pain in the chest and back, convulsions, complete weakness and a dizzy feeling, loss of hearing and speech, and sometimes unconsciousness. Usually, these symptoms will occur either in the water or immediately following the dive. It can be a reaction delayed from thirty minutes to ten hours or more, depending on the diver's condition and his exact decompression rate.

Treatment in a pressure chamber returns the diver, artificially, to the depth to which he dove, and gradually brings him to sea level pressure. Pressure is applied to his body in this chamber until the nitrogen bubbles are reduced sufficiently for the blood stream to absorb them. Then, during the slow decompression, the death-dealing bubbles can flow out of the lungs naturally, at a constant rate of flow, just as they would during a natural ascent in accordance with the decompression tables.

If a decompression chamber is not immediately available, which is the case in most isolated diving areas, an on-the-scene remedy can be put into use. The diver, upon surfacing, should immediately get into harness with another breathing device and descend to the deepest depth of his dive. He will begin to feel better as he decompresses, and if another diver is available with a breathing lung, he should accompany the stricken man as a security measure.

Depths of forty feet or less do not require decompression. Beyond this depth, which is the U.S. Navy standard, it is important to know the amount of time a diver has spent on the bottom in order to calculate the time of decompression in ascending. A working depth gauge and a waterproof watch now become important pieces of lifesaving equipment. Important, too, is the diver's judgment in saving sufficient air in his tanks to allow for slow decompression.

Following are the official United States Navy Decompression Tables. Where the accumulated time on the ocean bottom exceeds a time span shown in the number "2" column, the next greater time should be used. Time is measured by totaling the time spent in descending plus the time spent on the bottom. Where the depth of the dive is not shown in the tables, the next greater depth should be used.

How does a diver know how long to decompress and at what level? Do all divers memorize the long tables for each depth from forty to three hundred feet? Not likely, and divers usually have no idea to what depth they will dive, so pre-calculated decompression stops are almost impossible to figure unless a dive is made to a known depth.

A recommended practice is to have the Navy decompression table typed in large letters on two sheets of paper placed back to back, then laminated together with plastic whose edges are sealed, making the unit watertight. The diver's waterproof watch tells him the length of time he's

UNITED STATES NAVY DECOMPRESSION TABLES

(for Compressed Air)

1	2	3									4	5
		Stops (feet and minutes)									Sum of times at various	Approximate total decompression
Depth of dive (feet)	Time on bottom (minutes)	Feet 90	Feet 80	Feet 70	Feet 60	Feet 50	Feet 40	Feet 30	Feet 20	Feet 10	stops (minutes)	time (minutes)
40....	120	....	....	....	....	....	....	....	....	0	0	2
40....	180	....	....	....	....	....	....	....	....	2	2	4
40....	Opt.* 240	....	....	....	....	....	....	....	....	4	4	6
40....	300	....	....	....	....	....	....	....	....	6	6	8
50....	78	....	....	....	....	....	....	....	....	0	0	2
50....	120	....	....	....	....	....	....	....	....	2	2	5
50....	Opt.* 190	....	....	....	....	....	....	....	....	9	9	12
50....	300	....	....	....	....	....	....	....	....	12	12	15
60....	55	....	....	....	....	....	....	....	....	0	0	3
60....	75	....	....	....	....	....	....	....	....	2	2	5
60....	110	....	....	....	....	....	....	....	....	13	13	16
60....	Opt.* 150	....	....	....	....	....	....	....	5	15	20	24
60....	180	....	....	....	....	....	....	....	7	16	23	27
60....	210	....	....	....	....	....	....	....	8	18	26	30
70....	43	....	....	....	....	....	....	....	....	0	0	3
70....	60	....	....	....	....	....	....	....	....	4	4	8
70....	90	....	....	....	....	....	....	....	4	16	20	24
70....	Opt.* 120	....	....	....	....	....	....	....	13	16	29	33
70....	150	....	....	....	....	....	....	....	18	21	39	43
70....	180	....	....	....	....	....	....	....	21	32	53	57
80....	35	....	....	....	....	....	....	....	....	0	0	3
80....	50	....	....	....	....	....	....	....	....	6	6	10
80....	70	....	....	....	....	....	....	....	6	16	22	27
80....	100	....	....	....	....	....	....	....	20	16	36	41
80....	Opt.* 115	....	....	....	....	....	....	....	22	26	48	53
80....	150	....	....	....	....	....	....	....	28	29	57	62
90....	30	....	....	....	....	....	....	....	....	0	0	4
90....	45	....	....	....	....	....	....	....	....	6	6	10
90....	60	....	....	....	....	....	....	....	9	16	25	30
90....	75	....	....	....	....	....	....	....	18	14	32	37
90....	Opt.* 95	....	....	....	....	....	....	2	27	21	50	56
90....	130	....	....	....	....	....	....	9	27	29	65	71
100....	25	....	....	....	....	....	....	....	....	0	0	4
100....	40	....	....	....	....	....	....	....	....	12	12	17
100....	60	....	....	....	....	....	....	....	18	16	34	39
100....	75	....	....	....	....	....	....	....	27	21	48	53
100....	Opt.* 85	....	....	....	....	....	....	6	28	21	55	61
100....	90	....	....	....	....	....	....	8	27	24	59	65
100....	120	....	....	....	....	....	....	17	28	48	93	99
110....	20	....	....	....	....	....	....	....	....	0	0	5
110....	35	....	....	....	....	....	....	....	....	12	12	17
110....	55	....	....	....	....	....	....	....	22	21	43	49
110....	Opt.* 75	....	....	....	....	....	....	14	27	37	78	84
110....	105	....	....	....	....	....	2	22	29	50	103	110
120....	18	....	....	....	....	....	....	....	....	0	0	5
120....	30	....	....	....	....	....	....	....	....	11	11	17
120....	45	....	....	....	....	....	....	....	18	21	39	45

1	2	3										4	5
	Time on	Stops (feet and minutes)										*Sum of times at various stops*	*Approximate total decompression time*
Depth of dive (feet)	*bottom (minutes)*	*Feet 90*	*Feet 80*	*Feet 70*	*Feet 60*	*Feet 50*	*Feet 40*	*Feet 30*	*Feet 20*	*Feet 10*		*(minutes)*	*(minutes)*
120....	Opt.* 65							13	28	32		73	80
120....	100						5	22	27	69		123	130
130....	15											0	5
130....	35								11	15		26	32
130....	52							6	28	28		62	69
130....	Opt.* 60							13	28	28		69	76
130....	90						9	22	28	69		128	136
140....	15									4		4	10
140....	30								8	21		29	36
140....	45							5	27.	27		59	67
140....	Opt.* 55							15	28	32		75	82
140....	85						14	22	32	69		137	145
150....	15									7		7	14
150....	30								13	21		34	41
150....	38								28	30		58	65
150....	Opt.* 50							16	28	32		76	84
150....	80						18	23	32	69		141	150
160....	15									9		9	16
160....	34								27	28		55	63
160....	Opt.* 45							17	28	43		88	96
160....	75					3	19	23	34	68		147	156
170....	15									11		11	18
170....	30								24	27		51	59
170....	Opt.* 40							19	28	46		93	102
170....	75					9	19	23	38	68		157	167
185....	15									25		25	33
185....	26								24	37		61	70
185....	Opt.* 35							19	28	46		93	102
185....	65				18	18	23	37	65	51		212	223
200....	15									32		32	41
200....	23								23	37		60	69
200....	Opt.* 35							22	28	46		96	106
200....	60			5	18	18	23	37	65	51		217	229
210....	15									35		35	44
210....	Opt.* 30						5	16	28	40		89	100
210....	55			6	18	18	23	37	65	51		218	231
225....	15								6	35		41	51
225....	Opt.* 27						22	26	35	48		131	143
225....	60			13	18	18	23	47	65	83		267	280
250....	15								17	37		54	66
250....	Opt.* 25					2	23	26	35	51		137	150
250....	50		12	14	17	19	29	49	65	83		288	303
300....	12								20	37		57	70
300....	Opt.* 20					9	23	26	35	51		144	159
300....	45	6	14	15	17	18	31	49	65	83		298	315

* These are the optimum exposure times for each depth which represent the best balance between length of work period and amount of useful work for the average diver. Exposure beyond these times is permitted only under special conditions.

been under, and his depth gauge reveals the deepest dive. A quick check against the tables, and he knows where he must begin decompressing and the length of time at each stage. If he rises no faster than twenty-five feet per minute, he'll be in good condition when he surfaces.

Unfortunately, there is no deviation from all these good rules of survival. One man's blood, tissues, and cells are not stronger than another's to the point where these rules can apply to one and not to the other. If one must dive, then the rules must first be learned. If not, the only other course is to have a paid-up insurance policy.

Carbon monoxide poisoning. Victims of carbon monoxide are usually found lying on the floor of a closed garage or in a running car whose windows are closed. One doesn't think of this as asphyxiation beneath the seas, but it certainly happens. And when it happens, it's the result of careless filling of compressed air cylinders. The air in the tank was improperly filtered, permitting the exhaust fumes of a gasoline engine to enter the compressed breathing air. Small quantities of monoxide are not fatal, but under pressure, just as in the case of carbon dioxide, small amounts of this odorless, colorless gas increase in volume and become fatal to the diver.

The best cure is prevention. Compressors should be lubricated with a mixture of soap and water instead of lubricants usually used, and the exhaust pipe assembly should be run to an external source away from the compressor proper. If monoxide poisoning occurs, a physician should be called immediately, and oxygen should be administered if available.

Nitrogen narcosis. This temporary affliction of breathing nitrogen under extreme pressures in excess of 150 feet, but usually closer to two hundred, while using compressed air, has been described previously. In the interest of safety, it is recommended that one or more strong-willed and experienced divers accompany anyone seeking to establish a diving record in depths that would bring on this little known deep-dive effect. Experiments are still being conducted that are delving into deep descents with compressed air.

A PARTNER IS BEST FOR UNDERWATER ACTIVITIES

This is a whole chapter in the art of safety, and perhaps one of the most important single elements in underwater swimming: going down with at least one companion. In lung diving, team play is a must. Early in contemporary diving, Cousteau and his friend Frederic Dumas learned the value of having a man handy when an emergency arose. Dumas was working on the wrecked Dalton, alone and one hundred feet deep. He very nearly cut his breathing tube on a pipe covered with razor-sharp clams. It was established then that team diving would be the system thereafter, even among these advanced experts.

A tangled speargun line, a cramp, sweeping under-water currents, a hopeless tangle of abandoned fishing nets on wrecks, decayed wrecks, kelp entanglement, loss of air from breathing tanks, or stoppage of air from surface lines—these and many other emergent causes can be reason enough to be swimming with a companion. The assurance of a friend in the water makes underwater exploration that much lighter. A shark isn't considered as serious a threat, even to one inexperienced with shark contact, if there is a companion or three in the water at the time. Sharks and other predators, too, fear larger numbers and will, even if bent on attack, think twice and often will beat a hasty retreat.

In exploring a wreck off the coast of La Guaira, Venezuela, it was wise that a group of divers were together. One lung man entered the hold of a freighter through the hatch. His weight on the rotted planking suddenly caved in the superstructure, making a shambles of the area in which he disappeared. Masses of wreckage descended upon him. He was hopelessly trapped, but only for a minute. Four of us immediately began clawing at the wreck, tossing off the debris. We located our companion, unconscious, in what was at one time the hold. A beam had gashed his head. His mouthpiece was dangling. We picked up his limp form and began to surface, and fortunately we were only in some thirty-five feet of water, which required no decompression. Artificial respiration saved the diver, but had he been exploring the wreck alone, he would not have survived.

The greed for gold, in another instance, led an experienced diver to seek his fortune alone. From last reports he was still seeking, but his methods are not the recommended procedure.

Off the Isle of Pines, an island some thirty miles southwest of Cuba, a diver went in quest of a wreck known to have carried a shipment of gold more than two centuries ago. He used a portable air compressor, air hose, and mask. The compressor was unattended, and he was searching in waters varying from thirty feet to eighty. At this depth, a loose clamp on the hose connection would "squeeze" him to death, and he would have no one to offer assistance. If he had run out of fuel, or the compressor had failed, a cleverly attached reserve air tank would have provided sufficient air for his ascent. But if the hose had fallen off the outlet pipe—and that has been known to happen—he would still be in eighty feet of water, alone with his gold.

What is the best advice one can offer a diver? There is no substitute for common sense and good judgment.

~~~~~~~~~~~~~~~~~~~~~~~~~~~~~~~~~~~~ **5**

Preparation for the Plunge

BEGINNERS IN THE SPORT of underwater swimming
have much to learn. Not only must they learn to enjoy themselves, they must also learn to survive. The seas, in addition to
being a source of enjoyment, always hold the threat of death.
Thousands of drownings annually could be avoided if sufficient forethought as to water survival could be encouraged.
The American Red Cross, YMCA's, and thousands of schools
that have water safety programs offer many opportunities for
everyone to learn how to swim and to save the lives of others.

Advance knowledge of swimming and floating is necessary for all skin divers. Underwater swimming takes less pro-
ficiency in swimming than surface water sports require because the underwater man is naturally suspended in water and
can move about more easily. But once he breaks surface,
loaded with heavy equipment his surface counterpart doesn't

carry, he had better know how to swim to his craft or to the beach if he is to survive.

TAKE A DEEP BREATH

Once swimming is mastered, underwater activity will come easy. How then does one begin?

One begins in a swimming pool or in shallow water, always in the company of a competent swimmer, preferably an experienced underwater diver. The most important thing about the underwater is to learn your equipment, for depending on it, one survives or one perishes. The diver perishes when, because of panic, he cannot control himself or his equipment.

A lung diver in Florida waters ran out of air in thirty feet of water one morning and immediately began to panic. He could not manage the release of his lead belt, which would have allowed him to float to the surface. He froze on the bottom and passed out. Fortunately, his companions saw his plight and brought him to the surface. Later, he confessed that he did not think to shift over to the reserve supply of air in his tank. The very fact that he could not breathe for a moment petrified him.

Under competent supervision, everything underwater comes easy. The mask is adjusted until it sits properly on the face. The snorkel becomes an aid to breathing, keeping one on the surface longer without tiring. The student soon learns to dive with a snorkel. The point is, you hold your breath during the dive; you don't keep breathing. Then, when you surface again, you expel the water from the top part of the snorkel and resume breathing. Without this simple instruction, a diver us-

ing a snorkel could easily swallow mouthfuls of water unnecessarily and thus pick up a waterlogged prejudice against
this useful device.

Underwater diving is not complicated, but one must
conform to the principles set down. There is no deviation.
Nature has somehow taught us the right and wrong ways of
doing things. Fortunately, it is instinctive for human beings
to exhale immediately upon breaking the surface following
a dive—and then to take a fresh breath. As we ascend, the
remaining air in our lungs expands. Therefore, never *hold
your breath in ascending, whether with or without lung
equipment*—but especially with lung equipment. Unless the
air in your lungs is released, the delicate lung tissues can be
ruptured.

The same applies to diving. *Never hold your breath on a
dive.* Gradually release the air in your lungs as you dive,
keeping a small amount for your ascent which should be *completely* released upon surfacing.

MAKING LIKE A FISH

The very existence of a human underwater is complicated. So much strange knowledge must be considered. But
the most applicable rule of all is common sense. To spear a
fish in this strange world will only remain strange until the
diver learns the lore of his new environment. When he learns
sub-surface life and applies his own good judgment to it, he
becomes a knowledgeable man of the underwater.

After entering the water as tenderly as one walks on thin
ice over a frozen lake, the most logical underwater stroke is
either the dog paddle or the breast stroke. If the hands are

loaded with gear, the finned feet will propel the diver any-where underwater—up, down, into a barrel role, figure-eight —almost anything a small plane can do. You are an airplane underwater, free to float and glide and skid. Calm, gentle kicks of the fins will do the job best. Speed swimming strokes will tire out the heartiest of divers in short order.

Practice in using flippers is important. They give the diver tremendous speed, never before attained without them. But in using fins, foot and ankle muscles that are otherwise in-active come into severe play, so caution and slow acclimation to these swimming aides is recommended. Foot or leg cramps can easily beset the diver who, with flippers on his ankles for the first time, decides to swim several hundred yards in one burst of energy.

If we entered the water as in a crushing crescendo, we would scare the fins off the fish. It follows then, that there is a correct way of entering the water.

The recent underwater film, *Under the Red Sea*, pro-duced and directed by veteran diver Hans Hass, showed a novel and quite interesting method of entry. Two of his divers, fully equipped, would roll backwards from the gun-whale of their boat. That was a photogenic entry but not any way to enter the water. It scares fish, not only in the immedi-ate vicinity but for some distance around. And the divers could lose their masks from the force of impact.

A recommended method is to slide into the water from a boat feet first. An upward, pushing motion of the hands will take you into deeper water. Or, as soon as the head has cleared the surface, bend forward from the waist at about a forty-five degree angle and kick your fins in an undulating fashion. You'll go down without the use of your hands, which could be carrying a spear, camera, speciman bottle, or other gear.

If you want to get to the bottom quickly from a floating position on the surface, bend at the waist as a duck bends before diving. Start downward. Your legs and finned feet will be above water momentarily. At that moment begin a furious kick which will give you power and speed downward. Keep kicking till you've reached bottom.

An even quicker way to get to the bottom is to enter the water holding a heavy metal or stone weight at the waist. This method is not recommended for beginners

A check of all equipment is a "must" before entering any body of water. If using a small boat, a ladder is recommended. If from a skiff, simply ease yourself into the water and look around immediately. Sudden lunges into the water oftentime bring charging barracudas and sharks. The splash scares them and they attack. Also, be careful of the anchor line and boat propellers.

A rocky shore indicates rocks under the water—a good locale for fish. If entering the water from shore, get a clear picture of the calmest water away from rocks and breakers. Note the set of any currents. Work with currents rather than against them. It conserves energy. Walk into a calm surf and descend gradually, testing all equipment before reaching deep water. Spear guns should be uncocked until deep water is reached. There is always danger to companions and to oneself when carrying loaded guns, since undertow or an unseen breaker can easily topple over the diver loaded with gear.

Underwater, breathe normally. Be alert. Keep close to your companions. Take in your environment and enjoy it, but take it in moderation. When fatigue or cold creeps over you, look around for your boat or the nearest shore. Underwater fatigue comes more quickly than on land, especially when one is not accustomed to this new life, and will suddenly render a diver weak and helpless. To enjoy another dive, it's best to get out of the water before any tired feeling creeps over you.

When surfacing, watch what's overhead. A whirling outboard or inboard motor can easily be heard and avoided. A boat or dock overhead can be a menace if the diver floats head-first into it without looking. Break water and look for your boat, floating rubber tube, or the nearest shoreline. Make for it. If there is a considerable distance to swim, you made a serious error.

FORTY-FIVE TIPS ON LUNG DIVING

Breathing lungs are safe and sane pieces of equipment that have made the undersea as close to us as our own backyards. But it must be reiterated: learn your equipment thoroughly.

Here are some simple rules and observations.

1. The best lungs are those with a reserve air-supply feature that warns the diver when his main tank or tanks are out of air. A mechanical lever is actuated, causing the reserve supply to flow freely until the diver surfaces. A new regulator, recently marketed, features a built-in reserves, requiring no mechanical switch-over. When the air in the tank reaches a danger level, the diver feels restraint in breathing. This check point tells him to begin rising immediately. During the rise, sufficient air is supplied to reach the surface.

2. All tanks should be given an annual hydrostatic test for leakage and checked every four years for corrosion.

3. Because of extreme increases in temperature while refilling tanks, it is advisable to submerge them in cold water during the refilling process.

4. Losing a mouthpiece underwater should not be a great hazard to the diver who has checked himself out in controlled open waters or in a swimming pool. Water will immediately fill the rubber hoses. To get the water out of these hoses simply lift the mouthpiece above the level of the regulator and the pressure will open the air valve. Air will then force the water out of the intake hose. Now replace the mouthpiece, roll over on the left side, and take in a few short breaths of air through the cleared tube. Blow out the exhaust tube and everything returns to normal.

Divers have been known to panic in like situations. But there's no reason for it. Staged rehearsals of lost mouthpieces, first in swimming pools, then in open water, with other lung divers in attendance, will soon make this maneuver commonplace, even in the deepest waters. But as a last resort, if the inhalation tube does not clear when raised above the regulator, don't play with it, for the amount of air remaining in the lungs is small. Get rid of the lead belt and even the lung by unleashing both quick-release buckles, and swim for the surface. Make the ascent as slowly as possible, exhaling the remaining air in the lungs. Immediately, upon breaking surface, *exhale*, then take a deep breath. *Relax*, and get out of the water.

5. Weights and neutral buoyancy go hand in hand with lungs. The more weight a diver carries, the faster he will descend and conversely, the more difficult it will be to surface. The point of neutral buoyancy is that point below the surface where a diver, fully equipped, will be suspended as though weightless, like a helium-filled balloon just before it starts down.

(Don Ollis–Black Star)

Perhaps the friendliest of all water mammals is the sea lion—a happy, intelligent, and personable underwater playmate and companion. Off the island of Santa Cruz in the Galapagos group, photographer Don Ollis captured, in this picture of sea lions cavorting, something that many marine biologists had never before realized: principally that sea lions swim on their sides with their heads twisted sideways.

(Above) *A baby sea lion is the idol of the bull sea lion. Bulls prote*
pups and females alike with their lives. Ollis filmed the pups when the
were two months old—which brought the bulls charging when t
divers got too near their offspring. But after a week of photograph
even the bulls relented and became friendly. A baby lion rests here o
a lava rock for a close-up, showing his baby-like face. (Below) Papa s
lion. The bull of the flock poses majestically for his portrait against
background of spiny black angel fish. Sea lions swim by gyrating the
bodies and by using their streamlined flippers for locomotion.

(Above) *An Aqua Scooter is lowered from the deck of the
Calypso. This ship, outfitted for scientific research, has a
specially designed bow that has welded to it a 32-inch steel
sleeve, beginning at the deckline and extending eight feet
below the waterline. The base of the sleeve has glass ports
which are used for underwater filming.*

(Left) *A lung diver rides astride a giant turtle while his companion travels forth on the scooter, pitting reptile and man-made devices for underwater speed.*
(Below) *Divers are positioning underwater light cables and reflectors that house 6,000-watt flood lamps. More than 5,000 dives were made during the filming of* The Silent World, *which was directed by Cousteau assisted by Louis Malle.*

(From *The Silent World*)

(From *The Silent World*)

(Above) *Men of the Calypso prepare to haul the steel anti-shark cage—used successfully by the underwater cameramen when some thirty sharks attacked a dead sperm whale tied to the side of the ship. Photographers worked in the cage over 13,000 feet of water, held to safety only by a wire rope attached to the ship's winch. They shot color footage through the open door of the cage.*

This close-up of a shark, with another in the immediate background, was shot through the open door of the steel anti-shark cage. It shows the proximity of the cameramen to the shark during the free-for-all on the dead whale. The cage was bumped several times during the filming, each time swaying dangerously over the abyss.

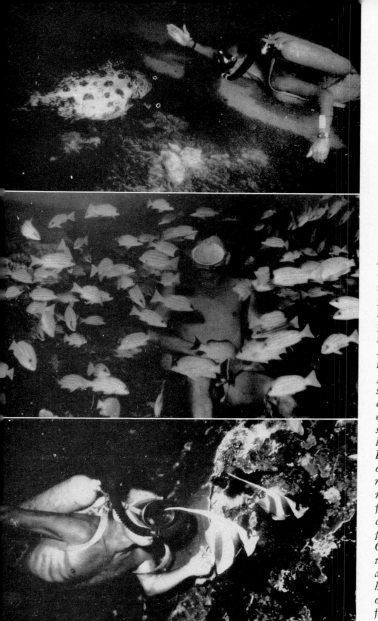

(Top) *Louis Malle plays with the friendly 80-pound spotted grouper who became the ship's underwater mascot and later became a nuisance. He was fed by the divers and accompanied them wherever they went until he was finally jailed in the anti-shark cage for interfering with the film scenes.* (Center) *Off Assumption Reef in the Indian Ocean, Jean Delmas, Calypso diving equipment chief, feeds a school of hungry fish while sitting on the ocean bottom.* (Bottom) *Frederic Dumas, one of the world's foremost free divers with more than 10,000 free descents to his credit, takes time to play in the Indian Ocean with two fish that resemble our angel fish. Dumas holds the world record descent of 307 feet on compressed air.*

(From *The Silent World*)

This is a rare scene: a sting ray quietly posing on the ocean floor for its portrait. Professor John F. Storr is shooting the portrait while the author is taking a picture of them both. The marine biology professor is using a Desco Mask unit and is supplied air from a portable surface compressor. The black hose to the right of the professor supplies the air, and he adjusts his own air input valve on the side of the mask.

(John Tassos)

(John Tassos)

(Top) *A dive* *swims to the barre* *ocean bottom wit* *knife in hand. Stin* *ray makes excellen* *shark bait.* (Center *Instead of knifing* *the diver grabs th* *sting ray at the ti* *of its tail and* *pulled along the bot* *tom by the powerfu* *undulating wings o* *the ray.* (Bottom *The diver is carefu* *not to get near the* *barbs at the base o* *the sting ray's tail—* *barbs that can inflic* *a painful injury* *Contrary to hearsay* *the sting ray's sting* *is not poisonous, and* *the ray is one of the* *most timid of the* *giant underwater* *creatures. It's cousin,* *the manta ray, who* *weighs many tons* *and whose wings* *spread more than* *twenty feet, is a veg-* *etarian.*

Another diver maneuvers a giant sting ray into perfect position to show its gills and mouth. The mouth has hundreds of little depressed teeth that act as a crushing plate. The gills expel water and the ray's underside is soft and fleshy.

(Carroll Seghers—Black Star)

The sting ray is positioned to show the sting at the base of the tail—a cluster of one, two, and sometimes three saw-edged spines that are its only weapon of defense. Spiracles in the upper section are intake for water when the ray is lying on the sandy ocean bottom, a customary habit. Otherwise the ray takes in water through the mouth.

(Right) *Night shark photography takes more than ability—it takes guts. When the picture was made, this eight-foot ground shark was held with hook and line, shown to the left of its head. (Below) A giant Galapagos brown shark thrashes violently against the steel gaff in the black waters as he is boated.*

(Don Ollis—Black Star)

(Don Ollis—Black Star)

(Top) *The gaffed hammerhead shark is named for the peculiar shape of the lobes that protrude beyond its body proper. At the extreme ends of either lobe are the shark's eyes; the lobes on a giant hammerhead have measured as much as three feet. The head is also known to be used as an effective battering ram. (Bottom) The sand shark dates back to the Cretaceous period, and when cornered this cold-blooded fish will attack viciously. The sand shark is easily recognized by its elongated, depressed snout and two dorsal fins, both about equal in size.*

(John Tassos)

(Right) *A lung diver floats through the opening of an underwater cave, silhouetted against the sun's penetrating ultra-violet rays. Scenes like these make underwater exploration seem like diving through unexplored space.* (Below) *This unusual coral growth resembles a giant dinosaur with growing plants on its back. A lung diver, approaching from the floor of the ocean, leaves a telltale stream of air bubbles from his compressed air tank.*

(H. Broussard)

(Philip Nash and Gustav Dalla Valle)

Coral normally has a full register of colors but loses color values to the diver's normal vision in the deep abyss, where everything appears a musty green-blue or dark purple. Reds photograph black at fifty feet. Artificial light at the deepest dive ever made by free divers has recently revealed the full color that nature gave the coral reefs of the tropics.

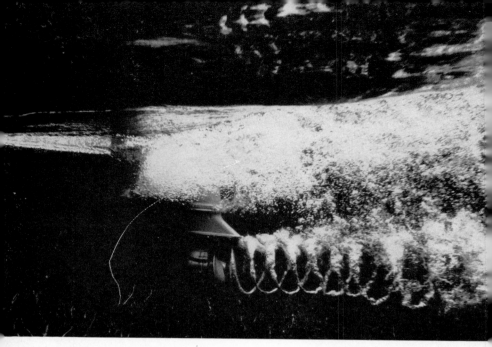

The whirling blade of an outboard propeller produces strange under-water patterns for the camera fan. Carroll Seghers of Miami patiently experimented for hours with a moving outboard motor, producing a beaded upper layer of foam and a series of circles from the blade in the lower portion.

A still and motion picture photographer pose an underwater model for visiting Florida tourists, who watch the activity through sunken ports and glass-bottom boats.

(Silver Springs, Florida)

Divers, especially cameramen and others who carry heavy equipment, must adjust their weight so neutral buoyancy comes at the level where they want to work, in order to free their hands. The neutral position will vary, depending upon the diver's size, weight, lung capacity, extra displacement due to equipment being carried, rubber suits, the amount of lead weights being carried, and even the diver's degree of relaxation. The amount of lead ballast added to, or removed from, the belt will soon determine the neutral position. For shallow diving, this position is important, as the diver is free to shoot pictures, explore reefs or caves, take samples of coral or sea shells or participate in any underwater activity.

In lung diving the neutral position will become higher as the air is used up, because the diver's load lightens, air having weight. The rise of the point of equilibrium will vary, depending upon the size of the tanks the diver is wearing. Allow for this rise. After finding the neutral buoyancy point, increase the lead weights slightly so that a slight "negative buoyancy" is in effect. This negative buoyancy will gradually give way to positive bouyancy as air is breathed out of the tank.

6. Weights and lungs can, at times, have what might be called negative value. When either becomes dangerous dead weight and has to be ditched, the one and only method is to unleash a quick release strap that will shed them both in less than four seconds. This special releasing harness should be properly adjusted before each dive, and should be the kind that requires the use of only one hand to operate.

On my first dive with an Aqua-Lung, I was entranced with the bottom of Soldier's Key in Miami. In those days a lung was an uncommon piece of equipment, and the safety education was not stressed as it is today. My friends gave me a brief indoctrination course in the lung's use but failed to tell me about adjusting a quick-release hitch on the lead belt or the lung harness. They went off to the deeps while I treaded water in the shallows at thirty feet, enjoying the underwater sights. Not knowing better, I breathed heavily and strenuously. In about twenty-five minutes I was out of air, while sitting on a rock thirty feet deep. The lung I was wearing had no safety reserve air supply. This feature had not been introduced yet.

My immediate and correct reaction was to get out of there. I tried to loosen the lead belt, but it would not give. I fumbled. The remaining air in my lungs was slowly running out. I ditched my gun, sprang from the bottom, and began pushing myself to the surface. My lungs were at the bursting point.

When I finally made surface I blew out the mouthpiece and breathed deeply, but then I sank back about five feet. I was weak from struggling, and now, loaded down with a lung and a stuck lead belt, I was struggling for survival with no assistance in sight. I rose to the surface again. The boat was anchored about 60 yards away, unattended. I talked myself out of panic, but the hitch in the belt stuck, and I went down again.

Finally it parted, on my fifth surfacing attempt, and I dropped it like fused dynamite. The hitch in the lung harness still refused to give. It was watersoaked and tight against the metal rings. I was exhausted. No one had told me about floating on my back to help float the tanks, but I instinctively tried it and with powerful kicks of my fins, I reached the speedboat. All this taught me the valuable lesson of using equipment that was positioned for quick-ditching in times of emergency. It was a lesson well learned and one every diver using such equipment should learn before he ventures into water above his head.

7. The length of time a lung diver may remain underwater varies with the tank size and number of tanks he is carrying, with his degree of activity, and more important, with his manner of breathing. Does he use volumes of air needlessly or is he conservative? Is he easily excited underwater, or does he breathe normally, thus making the air in his tanks last longer?

At thirty-three feet, a cylinder of compressed air containing seventy cubic feet (2365 p.s.i.) can last a diver fifty minutes or thirty minutes, depending upon what he's doing and how he's breathing. At seventy-five feet, that same cylinder of air could last thirty-five minutes or only fifteen minutes. The deeper a diver goes the more outside pressure he is subjected to; and more air is required as one goes deeper. So depth itself substantially affects the length of air time on a tank. If the diver is struggling to thrust a crowbar under a sand-covered anchor, he'll use more air than if he were sitting on the anchor at the same depth, merely counting fish.

Temperature of the water, too, plays an important part in the amount of air breathed by a lung diver. Divers in tropical waters breathe less air at similar depths than do divers in the cold waters of Nova Scotia or Seattle.

8. On a first dive with a lung, start by holding to the gunwhale of the boat to test the lung, convincing yourself that it works. Surprisingly, it does, and breathing underwater is really simple. Slowly, then, grasp the anchor line and gradually descend, getting accustomed to the various depths. If the ears or nose should become stopped up, rise a

foot or more, blow gently through the nose with the face-plate of the mask tightly against the nose, and descend slowly again. In time, you will equalize to the pressure at all depths. Release the anchor line and scour the area. You are now free-diving, completely dependent on yourself, and it's a thrill incomparable with motion on the surface.

9. Fill air compressor tanks with certified air containing no impurities or stray lubricants, and fill oxygen bottles with pure oxygen.

10. Spend days, if necessary, in controlled waters, learn-ing all the ways of lung equipment.

11. Wear a rubber suit in waters below sixty-eight de-grees, mindful of the fact that it's colder in deeper waters.

12. Always, but always, dive with a companion, or sev-eral, especially when using lungs.

13. Do not enter the water with a defective lung. Have it checked and repaired.

14. The lung harness should feel comfortable.

15. Occasionally, when using a full face mask with cer-tain lung equipment, exhaled CO_2 accumulates in it. This gas is fatal. If a diver begins to feel the effect of this gas poisoning, he should surface immediately.

16. In ascending, don't be in a hurry. A good self-pacing method is to stay beneath your rising air bubbles.

17. Keep all items of equipment independent of one another. Don't let a lead belt impede the removal of the lung harness.

18. It's a good rule of thumb to pause at about ten feet from the surface in ascending from a dive deeper than thirty-three feet.

19. Breathe lightly and freely on descent. Holding one's breath on a dive will cause ear pain, possibly even burst the ear drum. If in pain, rise a few feet and equalize to that level.

20. It's so important to *exhale* steadily when ascending. The human lungs cannot stand the pressure of not exhaling.

21. Store cylinders in a cool, dry place when not in use, and wash out the lung in fresh water, dry it, and store it carefully.

22. Avoid eating before a lung dive. Gas-forming foods, especially garlic and other condiments, will make you sorry you ate them.

23. The lifesaving reserve air supply on a tank is useless unless the lever that releases it is closed before submerging. Check it before descending.

24. Don't remove a lung mouthpiece underwater unless you're ditching the gear, offering your air to a stricken companion, or changing air tanks.

25. Don't exert yourself unnecessarily, especially in water deeper than fifty feet.

26. If you have a heart or sinus condition, perforated ear drum, a cold, or just feel bad, keep out of the water, but especially away from lungs.

27. Always slip out of the lung harness and weights while still in the water, if you're getting into a boat.

28. If out of air, either swim on your back or ditch the lung and drag it to your boat or to shore.

29. Don't try for a lung diving record unless you know what you're doing and have a competent crew who are thoroughly checked out in each of their assignments.

30. A lung mouthpiece should be held firmly in the jaws. The lips should encompass the outer ridges, and the teeth should clamp down tightly on the ridges provided in the mouthpiece.

31. Above all, don't try to be a hero with your lung. It's only meant for survival underwater, not impossible tasks.

32. When a dry rubber suit is punctured, it will flood with water and add weight, losing buoyancy. The remedy is to get out of the water. If rising is difficult, drop the lead belt.

33. Don't fight a running underwater current. Swim with it and seek out your float gradually.

34. Learn to administer artificial respiration. Any Red Cross swimming instructor can assist you.

35. Get out of the water immediately following a brush with coral and clean the wounds. Coral cuts can cause severe infection.

36. When rescuing a companion who has exhausted his air supply, the diver with the useable air supply should turn over on his back. This position puts the regulator below the intake mouthpiece, insuring better and easier breathing for the stricken diver. It also keeps the intake rubber hose clear of water since the air in the tube will blow out any water that might seep into the tube. The stricken diver should float above the diver with air, and alternately, they could take a lungful of air as they rise together. Every diver should thoroughly practice this rescue procedure in shallow water.

37. Compressed air tanks should be filled with air, not oxygen.

38. A ditched lung tank makes an excellent float when empty. It also makes swimming easier, unless you've learned to float on your back with the harness intact.

39. Learn to replace the mouthpiece underwater. Practice ditching the lung in regulated water with two companions standing by. Raising the air intake hose and mouthpiece above the regulator will clear the hose. Take the mouthpiece between your lips and clear the exhaling tube. Continue normal breathing and slip into or out of the harness and lead belt. Master this ditching and refitting underwater, and you've gained confidence that cannot be equalled by any other activity.

40. Don't try to disassemble the regulator. It is your lifesaving equipment and should not be tampered with, except by factory service representatives.

41. Wash the breathing unit with fresh water after each use. Keep the regulator unit in place to avoid getting water into the high pressure valve, which fills the tank. Dry it carefully, and store it away with the same care as cameras, binoculars, and other precision instruments.

42. Fill tanks only at registered air-filling stations that offer certified pure air—air that does not show a trace of carbon monoxide from a badly-placed exhaust.

43. On entering the water, be careful the regulator or the fitting does not strike against a rock or coral. A damaged regulator could mean your life.

44. When surfacing in kelp-infested waters, especially in the tough ribbon kelp that spreads over the water's surface, be certain that, the tank and regulator do not entangle in it.

45. When eel grass covers lung divers, it often panics them. If they wait until the wave surge changes, the grass will sway in the opposite direction in a few seconds, uncovering them.

~~~~~~~~~~~~~~~~~~~~~~~~~~ 6

Basic Equipment for the Diver

EQUIPMENT WORKS ONLY in the hands of those who understand it. A welding torch, a typewriter, or a sewing needle is only as successful as the user can make it.

The same principle applies to underwater gear. In the hands of anyone who has been checked-out with it, it will respond exactly as the experts say it will—and as it does for them. Underwater equipment is a combination of two essentials: survival and protection. Neither can be minimized, and both must be learned thoroughly. Underwater gear is highly specialized, yet basically simple to use. It must be, since it is meant for survival in an unnatural element.

There is, however, some equipment that is unnecessary, but still used indiscriminately by swimmers and divers. In particular, there are ear plugs, which are useless and dangerous to the diver. One cannot equalize to descending pressure with ear plugs, and at great pressures the plugs can be pushed right into the ear, easily bursting the eardrums. If divers suffer when water enters their ears, they had best abstain from diving.

Underwater devotees have acquired a healthy respect for the simple, specialized gear that makes it possible for them to remain under the surface. As a fan recently said, "I put my lung and mask away after each use, almost with the same amount of care that I give to my wife. They're both important to me."

Equipment for the beginner is simple and compact. Each piece has a function, for a diver must travel as light as possible, carrying only essentials.

Basic equipment for the shallow diver: a mask and snorkel, a pair of rubber fins, and a knife.

Basic equipment for a lung diver: a mask, rubber fins, knife, lead belt with quick release, depth gauge, and an artificial breathing device.

These are basic. Many combinations of equipment, more or less than those described, are used by individual divers. The choice depends upon the diver, the water, and what the diver has in mind.

Use of this equipment and continued research by underwater club groups and manufacturing concerns are constantly revealing new and improved underwater gear. Present equipment is extremely satisfactory, but the future holds great prospects of improvement, especially with the artificial breathing devices.

Here are the most popular types of equipment in underwater today.

THE BASIC EQUIPMENT

Mask. This piece of equipment is considered the basic key to discovery of the underwater's wonders. It is the most significant, because without it, all the other underwater gear would be almost useless. The mask affords vision beneath the sea that equals our vision on land. It consists, basically, of a thick, unbreakable glass plate, which is set in soft rubber moulded to the contour of the face, with adjustable rubber straps to hold the mask to the face.

Wearing a mask, in many cases among beginners, eases the degree of fright. Vision with it is clear underwater instead of the blur a swimmer sees if he opens his eyes when not wearing one.

Naked eyes that are continually exposed to salt water whose salt content is around 3.2 per cent, like most ocean water, will soon smart and hurt. Eyes "sting" even with the flow of tears, whose salt content is less than half that of the average body of ocean.

There are many face coverings on the market. The most desirable cover the eyes and nose. Other types include goggles that cover the eyes alone, and masks that cover the entire face from eyes to chin. Some masks, with attached snorkel, cover up to the nose, while others cover the entire face. All are fine and depend upon the diver's choice, based on comfort and convenience in use.

The mask captures air between the face plate and the eyes, which is the secret of clear underwater vision. The desirable mask has a center layer of plastic, laminated to sheets of glass on either side, making the unit shatterproof. An underwater impact, therefore, will not harm the diver's eyes or face.

A cheap mask will give second-rate performance. It will not fit properly. It permits water to leak in. Air must be trapped tightly inside the mask, and the deeper one dives the more important that function becomes. The diver must then build his mask pressure up to the increased outside pressure by snorting extra air into the mask through his nose.

When water does leak into the mask, it must be expelled by one of two methods. The method practiced by most beginners is to surface and let the water out by lifting a tip of the mask from the face. Then a simple tightening of the rubber straps will usually remedy the leak. More experienced divers expel the water right then and there, underwater. How? It's simple. Tilt the head backward; the water, which is heavier than air, will sink to the bottom of the mask. As the mask is lifted slightly at the base one powerful snort will force the water out. Then the mask is pressed more firmly to the face, and the head strap tightened a bit to make the mask watertight.

All divers should test a mask for leakage before they enter the water. After it's firmly in place, they should try to inhale slowly through the nose. If air enters the mask, that means it will leak water later. To correct this measure, mould the mask to the face and readjust the straps.

Glasses can be worn with some underwater masks. A properly-fitted mask will permit it, but some more serious enthusiasts have their masks fitted with a prescription faceplate.

The one cardinal rule most underwater people soon learn is never to dive into the water while wearing a face mask. You can lose your mask and possibly even shatter the plate. The impact can also hurt the nose as the mask flies off.

There are two methods of keeping the faceplate from being fogged. Dip the mask into water, and rub the inner and outer surfaces of the glass with saliva or soap concentrate. Then rinse the mask and put it on.

While underwater, do not exhale into the mask unless it's necessary to equalize the pressure in a deep dive. Learn to exhale through the mouth. Hot breath on the mask has a tendency to fog the faceplate. Warm breath on a cold glass will produce the same result on land—try it on a window pane during the winter.

After each dive, it is a good idea to rinse the mask and any other piece of equipment in fresh water. Keep the mask in a cool, dry place. And when putting it away for the winter, sprinkle talcum powder on the rubber, and fill the mask with crumpled tissue paper. Salt water pits the rubber straps and the rubber skirt next to the face. Straps can be replaced, but when the skirt becomes pitted, it's time for a new mask.

Masks cost from about $2.95 to $6.95.

Fins. They're also called flippers, duck-feet, and web-bed-feet. Whatever the name, they're certainly useful. By making the feet more efficient swimming devices, they leave the diver's hands free, most of the time, to operate cameras or spearguns, collect tropical fish or shells, and to do any other job that comes along. A slow, methodical kick of the fins will maneuver the diver anywhere. Body turns steer the diver, and assistance from the hands, although useful, is actually unnecessary.

Fins have an amazingly noticeable effect on the underwater diver. He feels as graceful as a sea lion. He swims at almost the speed of a barracuda. He is untiring and forever moving. Polynesians and other natives in the South Pacific learned many years ago that palm fronds lashed to the feet with vines increased their speed in the water. Fins are merely a modern version of what these primitive natives worked out, probably as a result of noticing how fish swam.

Fins should fit properly and must be comfortable. Some divers prefer to wear wool socks with their flippers. It prevents chafing for those with sensitive feet. A tight fin will, at times, stop circulation of the blood in the feet. Loose-fitting fins will raise blisters.

A number of types of fins are on the market—hard rubber, soft rubber, long and short fins, fins that sink, and fins that float. The beginner is advised to get a short fin made of soft, flexible rubber. Leisurely kicking with such fins is easy and will not tire the diver too quickly. Fast, furious kicking will not only tire the diver but may cause an underwater cramp. The leg muscles not normally in use will knot. A quick massage will sometimes relieve the ache, but it is best for the beginner to get out of the water.

A useful and sensible kind of fin is one with a rubber bottom for the entire foot. This permits walking on rocks or coral without fear of cutting the heel. The rubber is also hard enough to resist the sharp needles of the spiny sea urchin. If for no other reason, beating the sea urchin at his own game is reason enough to wear a fin with a rubber bottom in waters where urchin live.

Fins will also send the diver down more quickly in a vertical dive. Powerful leg strokes, kicking in the same manner as in swimming, will send a diver down to new records faster. The longer the fin and the harder the rubber, the more power the diver can generate in his dives.

Fins, like masks, should be washed out in fresh water after each use and dusted with talcum when being stored for the season.

Fins cost from about $2.95 to $12.00.

Snorkel. This is an amazing little gadget. It is named for the schnörkel, the breather tube for submarines first used by the Dutch navy. Its job is to allow a person to keep his head under water indefinitely, breathing all the while. It is simply a rubber or plastic tube about twelve inches long, curved, with one end supplying air to the user and the other projecting above the water. (It would be nice if a snorkel could be five or six feet long, but pressure increases so rapidly under water that even a few feet down a diver cannot breathe surface air through a tube. He must carry his own air, or be fed compressed air to keep his insides pressurized, to meet the pressure of the water around him.)

The simplest snorkel is fitted to a mouthpiece held between the teeth, and the user breathes through his mouth. Snorkels are also permanently attached to masks that cover the eyes and nose and there are others that cover the entire face, in which case one breathes through the nose. Some snorkels have light ball or cork valves in the upper end, designed to close the passage if the swimmer momentarily dunks his head, bringing the tip below the surface.

Some divers find it difficult adjusting to a snorkel. It is really the most adaptable instrument the underwater diver can use. A man with a snorkel, whether it is attached to a mask or separate, can easily spend the day floating on the surface, head in the water, and snorkel extended above, looking at sea life, hunting ocean treasures, or counting fish for his local conservation society. And diving with a snorkel is no different than diving without one. Water is held back by the captured air in the tube, and when the diver surfaces again, he simply blows out the tube and resumes breathing. To get accustomed to the snorkel, it's advisable to try it out under controlled conditions before venturing out into deeper water.

In rocky or kelp-filled waters, a rubber snorkel that bends under impact is best. Rigid snorkels have a tendency to snag on kelp growths, protruding rocks, and coral heads. Impact can easily dislodge a mouth-held snorkel, or, when the snorkel is a part of the mask, could fill the mask with water or knock it off.

Snorkels cost up to about $5.00, masks with attached snorkel from about $6.95 up. Double-snorkel masks are more expensive than the single-snorkel type.

Knife. The knife has been described through the ages as man's most formidable weapon. It is useful underwater, but contrary to popular belief, the knife is *not primarily* used as a weapon of defense against monsters. There are a few recorded instances in which a knife saved the life of a diver pitted against a shark or moray, or other occasionally aggressive fish. But the knife is principally used as a tool: to cut kelp and seaweed; to pry up abalone; to poke at coral or at the wood of wrecks. In an emergency, it can cut a lead belt, and there are hundreds of other such uses. In nine years of diving, I have not had occasion to use my knife against a fish underwater. But its always there, stowed in a waterproof sheath.

The choice of a knife with a cork handle, so it will float, or a knife designed to sink is entirely the diver's. One diver off the California coast hit it lucky with a cork-handled knife. He was diving alone, in relatively shallow water. Wearing a one-tank lung, he swam through an extensive growth of kelp. About ten feet from the surface, he became hopelessly entangled in the vines. The barnacle-covered branches engulfed him. His wriggling and turning only entangled him more, twisting the rubber breathing tubes of the lung. Finally, the thrust of his powerful turns ripped the mouthpiece from his mouth. He was momentarily helpless. He reached for his knife and almost panicked: The sheath was empty. The knife had dropped out. Bewildered and frightened, he struggled and tore at the kelp with his hands. His lungs ached. Suddenly his cork-handled knife drifted into view before his eyes. Apparently it fell out lower down, and it was leisurely floating toward the surface. Several quick strokes of the blade and the kelp released him.

This experience only served to teach the diver that knives should be securely fastened. But had he used a steel-handled knife that sank when dropped, the outcome might have been disastrous. Does this mean all divers should wear both a sinkable and a floating knife? Hardly, but that might be an idea. Many divers swear by surplus U.S. Marine knives. They're a very reliable knife, and the point is sharpened on both sides.

Cost of a knife: anywhere from $1.98 to $18.00 and more depending on the make and construction.

Lung. Whetting of the appetite for underwater activity begins with the simple mask-and-flipper dive. Hanging suspended amid the wonders of the sub-surface world, there is no doubt but that the diver will marry the underwater. A snorkel may soon be added to the equipment, followed closely by other gear. Yet the dream of all devotees is to swim in deeper waters along with, and like, the fish. But without proper breathing equipment, there can be little prolonged fraternizing with fish.

One of the truly great contributions to underwater exploration and sport in the last decade or more is the invention of the self-contained "open-circuit" artificial breathing unit by Captain Cousteau and Emile Gagnan. Their experiments, which led to the development of the present Aqua-Lung (the most popular underwater lung in use today throughout the world), extended underwater sport and made exploration with self-contained breathing units possible. This lung, the basic idea of which has been copied by others in the United States and abroad, has opened brand new vistas. While the heavily-garbed, helmeted suit-diver of the past had mastered the waters beneath the surface, the Aqua-Lung and its contemporaries now simplified and expanded the diver's activities.

Whereas a heavily-equipped helmet used to be required for exploration or work in one atmosphere of water (thirty-three feet), skin divers, even without breathing equipment, now dive that deep with ease. Lung divers explore at that depth by the hour. One Florida diver remained on the bottom near that depth for a twenty-four hour virgil in 1953, to prove the enormous flexibility of diving equipment. His record has since been exceeded several times.

By the thousands, underwater fans are entering the water throughout the world. With air tanks made of steel on their person, they remain underwater for a half hour and longer before surfacing, a feat almost beyond imagination just a decade ago.

All a diving lung does is enable the diver to breathe air

while underwater. But that's tougher than it sounds. Since pressures increase as one descends, the lung must be able to supply air at a constant output at increasing pressures.

The more popular lungs have "demand" regulators. This means they can deliver air to a diver as he needs it, at varying depths. Since each thirty-three foot drop increases the pressure against a diver's body by another atmosphere, more air must be delivered to him. The deeper one works underwater, the shorter the duration of the dive, since the air in the steel tank is used up more rapidly. In ten feet of water or less, the standard Aqua-Lung tank, containing seventy cubic feet of air, will last an hour or more, depending upon the regularity of breath. At eighty to one hundred feet, the same tank will give a diver about twenty-five minutes of air, again depending upon how severe a strain he applies to the regulator, which in turn is determined by what he's doing. A diver gliding through one hundred foot waters, examining reef or kelp bottoms or collecting specimens, can remain at that depth longer than a diver who is fighting a holed-up jewfish.

As with any such invention, the lung, with its complicated purpose of supplying precious air to man in a strange world to which he does not belong, was not easy to develop. Captain Cousteau and his many associates worked long and hard to perfect a unit that would do the work of our lungs underwater. Simulating the air we breathe freely in shallow underwater is in itself a triumph, but in combination with combatting crushing pressures of the deeps, it is an almost herculean task. Ways and means had previously been sought for breathing underwater, but most met with failure. To carry a portable breathing tank on one's person seemed, for years, the most unlikely of tasks.

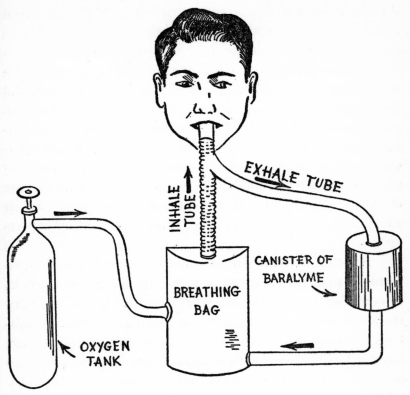

INHALE TUBE

EXHALE TUBE

CANISTER OF
BARALYME

BREATHING
BAG

OXYGEN
TANK

The "Closed Circuit" Principle

A second breathing unit, on the "closed circuit" principle, and not nearly as popular as the compressed air lung, is the re-breather type. The tank of this lung contains pure oxygen, which flows into a breather bag from which the diver inhales. He exhales carbon dioxide into a cannister containing a chemical—usually baralyme, a non-caustic, non-toxic chemical (homogeneous mixture of barium hydrate and calcium hydroxide compressed into cylindrical pellets, if anyone cares). The chemical removes the carbon dioxide from the exhaled breath. To the remaining oxygen, fresh oxygen is added from the tank as needed, and the air is "re-breathed." Air bubbles are not released into the water from a re-breather. Therefore, this unit, a favorite with the U.S. Navy Underwater Demolition Teams during World War II, does not leave a tell-tale trail of air bubbles to identify the location of the underwater diver. These breathing lungs are not recommended for amateurs. Toxic effects result from breathing concentrated oxygen below thirty-three feet. A manual adjustment of the oxygen intake valve must also be made by the diver as he descends and rises. Although this equipment has its advantages, as the Navy learned, it must be used by experts only.

Another extreme danger—and this unit is loaded with them—is to be sure to continue breathing in a complete cycle, or embolism will result. Another important "must"—empty the lungs and the breathing bag as much as possible immediately before descent. That removes most of the nitrogen. Pure oxygen breathed under two atmospheres of pressure is also capable of producing nausea, convulsions, and temporary blindness—all caused by oxygen poisoning. A diver seized with these symptoms is incapable of sustaining himself at times, and if diving alone, he may easily drown.

The thing to do is get anyone suffering with oxygen poisoning out of the water immediately, to breathe free air once more. There are usually no fatal aftereffects and the discomforts pass off several hours after exposure. Medical care should, nevertheless, be sought.

Deaths have been reported among amateurs who have been known to make homemade re-breather units. Of all the home workshop equipment that could be made for use in the underwater, a re-breather unit is the only one *not* recommended. The thread linking life and death is too thin. All it takes is a few drops of water in the cannister containing the chemicals that repurify the oxygen to cause death almost instantaneously. Carbon dioxide alone becomes a deadly poison. Three deaths in the Long Island Sound area have been caused by faulty homemade re-breather units. All could have been avoided if proper information had been sought before testing in deep water. Again, homemade breathing equipment is a hazard. Keep away from it.

A third piece of equipment for underwater breathing— not self-contained—consists of a mask and air hose. The diver wears a full face mask with air valve adjustment and is fed air from the surface air compressor at constant volume. He can control the amount of inflow by turning a valve at the side of the mask. The diver is, however, limited in movement to the length of air hose, usually sixty feet or less. This unit is primarily for shallow diving. It has been used without a surface attendant for the air compressor, although that is certainly *not recommended*.

One diver off the northeast coast of Haiti worked with a Desco mask of this sort on a salvage job for three months, completely unattended. He used a Navy surplus oxygen tank that held ten minutes' emergency air supply to which he often automatically transferred when his air compressor ran out of gasoline. He would then immediately begin to rise, knowing he had ten minutes' reserve air. He used ordinary rubber garden hose that floated away from the sharp coral reef near his working area. Air with such units should be supplied the diver from twenty to thirty pounds in excess of the water pressure at the level the diver is working.

With all these lung units, the usual underwater masks, fins, and other working equipment are used, except when using the surface-hose mask. Here, a regular mask is unnecessary, since the air hose is attached to the special mask itself.

A lung, under the best conditions, is dangerous unless its user has been thoroughly briefed in every facet of its operation and safety. In the hands of an expert the lung is one of the most useful undersurface pieces of equipment.

Cost of lungs: $129.95 to $250.00 or more.

OPTIONAL EQUIPMENT

In order to enjoy underwater swimming and to reduce its hazards there has been developed other equipment, some of it optional and some essential.

Depth gauge. Divers wear them like wrist watches. They continuously indicate the depth of a dive, usually to as deep as 220 feet. Cost: about $2.50 and up.

Compass. This piece of equipment is just as essential underwater as in the air or on land. It's simple to get lost in deep water, especially when a diver can't see in which direction the surface lies. Cost: about $10.00.

Glass-bottom bucket or "waterscope." This is not truly a piece of underwater equipment, since it's used on the surface, but underwater divers use it to examine the bottom before diving. It has many uses. Fishermen hunt turtles, lobsters, scallops, and other fish by peering through it. Lost property is sought with it. The tourist's standby, the glass-bottomed boat, is really a big bucket through which visitors look at submerged tropical plants and fish in many tourist havens of Florida, California, and Caribbean waters. Some do-it-yourself addicts make buckets from butter tubs and plate glass, with sealing or bee's wax to watertight the seams. Cost: From $2.00 to $12.00.

Flashlight. Here is a must item for deep divers, cave or wreck explorers, or divers who go into murky or disturbed waters where the visibility is poor. Suitable versions are standard two and three cell flashlights with watertight rubber covers. Cost: about $3.00.

Weight belt. This is a belt that carries lead ballast necessary for divers who use lungs. A one-hand, quick-release hitch is essential for the belt, which fits snugly around the waist. Many divers use surplus infantry cartridge belts whose pockets are filled with rectangles of poured lead. The hitch on this belt, however, requires use of both hands, and hands can be scarce in an emergency, so this belt is not recommended. Cost: About $5.95 and up.

Wristwatch. Many of the waterproof wrist watches on the market are actually waterproof enough for use underwater. Their most important function is to log time spent underwater for purposes of decompression. Cost: About $25.00 and up.

Rubber suit. For the diver who must—or who likes to—go into the water when it's cold, rubber suits have been developed. There are both "wet" and "dry" suits to fit the individual purpose. Water trapped between the skin and the suit helps retain heat when using the wet suit. The dry suit actually is watertight, and warm underclothes are worn with it. There also are do-it-yourself suits on the market, pre-cut to general builds, whose seams must be cemented together. These cemented suits are not as durable as the seamless. Cost: To about $60.00.

Air pressure gauge. This unit tests the amount of air pressure in a tank of air either before or after a dive. It's important to know the amount of air in a tank at all times. Cost: About $12.75.

Floating surface unit. These are a skin diver's constant companion. The Air Force surplus one-man rafts are excellent, but truck tire inner tubes also meet the test of practical diving. These floating palaces usually hold fish catches, spare equipment, reading matter, cameras, waterproofed film, tools, and sometimes a companion. One diver in the Florida Keys once took Lady Bunny, his cocker spaniel, spearfishing in a rubber raft. He kept filling the raft with lobster, many of which were still alive and flipping about wildly. Bunny added to the confusion aboard the raft, scrambling about, barking and clawing at the lobster. The dog-loving diver was coming up with another speared lobster when suddenly he was drenched with falling lobster, cocker spaniel, his lunch basket and extra spearing equipment. The commotion aboard the raft had ripped the bottom out, scattering its occupants and gear into Hawks Channel. Together man and dog swam the two miles to shore, towing their doughnut raft behind them.

Paddle boards, small skiffs, and dinghies are also used as surface units. All craft should be anchored in the area of diving with seaworthy anchors. Rubber rafts and inner tubes can be tied to anchored kelp or seaweed with nylon line, or can be anchored on the bottom with a light anchor in the open sea. One place not to tie up is on a piece of coral. Its jagged edges can easily cut the line; then wind and currents can drift the raft out of sight. When divers change locations they should also take their floating unit with them. It's comforting to know there's a boat or raft overhead at times.

Underwater bicycle. This contraption resembles a one-wheeled bicycle with airplane wings. The diver, with or without a lung, sits on the seat and peddles underwater. It saves swimming—but it also seems to defeat the whole idea of underwater swimming. It's available, but not very popular with skin divers. Cost: About $250.00.

Gloves. Hands should always be protected under water. Coral formations are sharp; lobster spines easily pierce unprotected hands; scale fish fins are razor-edged; and stinging coral burns for days if touched with the hands or any other part of the body. Sea urchins are a nuisance, and their spines, not unlike porcupine needles but twice as menacing, should be avoided. If they must be handled, it's best to wear a pair of gloves. Cotton work gloves are best suited. Leather gloves are slippery when wet. And, if gloves are in the spearman's way, he can always tuck them under his belt or inside his bathing trunks.

Portable air compressors. Divers on expeditions into isolated areas where no stationary air refill supply is available for lung tanks, can now bring along their own compressors. The Cornelius compressors, made to supply compressed air free from carbon dioxide, are available in several models. One unit supplies two cubic feet of air per minute and contains an integral twenty-seven volt DC electric motor, adapted for use aboard a boat with a 24–32 volt DC power source. Other units supply from 0.6 to 2. CFM of air, operating with AC current or independent gasoline engines, for dock-side or boat use. All units are portable. Costs: From $396.00 to $650.00.

Res-Q-Pak. These four-ounce mites are "musts" for underwater divers. They are vinylite floats capable of carrying

a diver and his equipment—a total weight up to 250 pounds—
to the surface and supporting him there. To operate, simply
squeeze the pack, which is usually clipped to a diver's bathing
trunks. A steel pin pricks a cartridge of highly compressed
CO_2, releasing the gas into the water wings. Cost: $2.98.

~~~~~~~~~~~~~~~~~~~~~~~~~~ **7**

The Spearfisherman and His Equipment

WITH THE TREND TO UNDERWATER FISHING has come a new group of weapons. Beside the gun, the bow and arrow, and the knife, there have been few other sporting weapons in use. The underwater gun is the first really new weapon to be introduced into the world of sport in generations.

The spear, with a shaft of wood and a harpoon head fashioned from flint and other stones, and later metal, was used many thousands of years ago for spearing fish in the sea, rivers, and lakes. We have since graduated to other more effective weapons for use on both land and underwater, but the spear still finds its place among undersea weapons.

As equipment for remaining underwater improved, and

as fishermen advanced farther into the deeps, they required speedier, more penetrating, and more effective weapons for spearing fish and for protection. Thus, there have been developed rubber slings, spring-powered guns, rubber-powered guns, gas-propelled guns and—from the looks of the new cartridge and powder guns and the formidable looking harpoons for killing larger predators—an underwater bazooka, or the equivalent in hitting power, may be invented next.

The underwater gun has proven its worth. It is now displayed beside the Winchesters, H. & H. Magnums, and the Remingtons in sporting goods stores, especially in diving areas.

Underwater weapons are divided into four main classes:
1. Hand-propelled spears and spearguns.
2. Spring-powered guns.
3. Rubber-powered guns.
4. Compressed-air-powered guns.

In each of these categories, several types of weapons are at the disposal of the hunter. Each has its own individual uses, recommended by the manufacturer and practiced by hunters, and each hunter seems to develop his own particular way of using them when attacking fish.

HAND-PROPELLED SPEARS AND SPEARGUNS

The most popular of this class—and for that matter, any class—is the sling. It is better known as the Hawaiian sling— a steel shaft from three to seven feet in length, propelled through a six to nine-inch piece of bamboo, a length of iron pipe, aluminum tubing, or even garden hose. The hunter pulls back an elastic made of inner tube or surgical rubber (the more acceptable of the two) and stretches as far back as possible. The farther back he pulls, the more power of propulsion he gathers, and the more penetrating power he generates. Most slings are made in the home workshops of underwater men. They are simple to construct and just as effective as the store-bought models that have cleaner lines. (There's one big difference—commercial models have no knots in the bamboo shooter.)

The steel shafts are made of beach-umbrella rods, flexible steel rolled stock, or stainless steel. These slings, simple as they may seem, are almost as effective as the more expensive and highly powered guns made of steel. In skilled hands they can equal the performance of bigger guns. The knowledgeable Pinder brothers of Miami use home-fashioned slings exclusively, and together the three Pinders have captured ten of forty-three record-breaking fish that the Florida Skin Diving Association lists on its books. Included in their fantastic collection of fish brought to bay with the simple hand-powered spear is an 804-pound jewfish, the only known sailfish ever speared, and a 337-pound tiger shark. During the 1954 AAU championships in the Florida Keys, the three Pinders won the meet by bringing to shore 281 pounds of fish with their simple spears, against competition with spring and rubber-powered guns of higher force and penetration.

The time it takes to load an underwater gun sometimes spells the difference between getting or losing a fish. With the simple sling guns, spearmen can load as they swim. In close quarters—in rocky or coral areas, or among ribbon kelp, which affords little room for maneuvering—the short sling is a more effective weapon. The long, unwieldy rubber or the still longer spring gun must be loaded, aimed, leveled, and fired. Also, when there's little time to aim at a fleeing fish, the sling works best. The experienced hunter has the spear ready at all times. A stretch of the rubber and the shaft is released instantaneously. There are no lines or reels. It takes a crafty underwater man with sharp stalking instincts and powerful swimming ability to get close enough for the kill with a Hawaiian sling. Amateurs fumble with it until one day they master its simplicity. Then they are able to compete with the masters.

Five youngsters in the Bahamas, none older than fourteen and the youngest only six, attacked and killed a six-foot sand shark with their home-styled slings. In relays of two, they dove on the shark with their barbless, sharpened umbrella rods and shot the shark in the gills. Seven spears hung from the mortally wounded shark in ninety seconds. The fourteen-year-old dove for the coup de grace, a knife tightly clenched in his youthful hand. He reached for the gill slits on the starboard side and tore vengefully with the steel blade. The shark was dead. It weighed more than the individual weight of three of the boys, and it was longer than any of them. More powerful guns in less experienced hands would not have done the big job these seasoned underwater kids accomplished. It's not the might, at times, but the manner. And in a strange water world, an ounce of know-how will outweigh pounds of brawn and daring.

Techniques vary with the individual and with the kind of gun used. The sling necessitates close proximity to the prey. A grouper, for instance, can be speared from above while hiding in his rocks—from below or on the same level, also. A silent dive to a hovering position above the fish will give the spearman a direct line-of-sight firing advantage. If attacking from below, a stealthy rise to the fish's level will bring the diver into a parallel firing position—a perfect spot for the sling. Dive or rise quietly. Avoid striking coral with the spear or splashing about wildly. Shoot for the gills or the head area, the vulnerable spots. And an important rule is never to leave a wounded fish in the water.

Another hand-propelled weapon is the ordinary spear, usually made with a wooden handle. The type of point is up to the fisherman. Single quarter-inch steel tines or double and triple tines are available. The handle length varies from five feet to ten. The object of this hand spear is to pin the fish, usually less than twenty pounds, to the bottom. A silent and undisturbed approach is essential with a hand spear, or the fish will get away.

This spear is a perfect fending weapon against sharks and moray eels, manta rays that career too closely in their glides, and giant jewfish that are too tough to tackle with this simple spear. Lobsters are perfect targets for the double and triple-tined spear. They are visible under rocks, antennae extended into view. Seasoned underwater lobster fishermen have learned to tickle the antennae with a spear. The lobster comes out of his hole, unaware of the next scene: Usually it's the frying pan or the pressure cooker.

The sea lance is another hand-propelled weapon, similar to the hand spear except that the lance is rubber powered. The shaft is ten and sometimes twelve feet long with a sharp steel point, barbed or not. It is weighted at the head to permit slight negative buoyancy and better penetration. The steel head is usually detachable. On impact, the steel head remains in the fish, breaking away from the shaft and held by a one hundred-pound test line or steel wire. The fish plays against the line, which tires it more easily. Too, the shaft could easily be broken by a twenty- or thirty-pounder.

A strange incident happened in shallow waters off the coast of Curaçao two summers ago. Two visiting divers were fishing with the spear sling. (A sort of bow-less bow and arrow with a strip of live rubber tied to the end of the spear shaft. To shoot the spear, the diver stretches the rubber and grips the shaft. At the proper instant, he releases the shaft and the spear flies through the water.) The two men were diving through the coral formations and became separated momentarily. One spied a hog fish of about twelve pounds and proceeded to stalk him.

Near the base of the reef at the entrance to some caves the diver released the spear and impaled the fish in the sand. The sudden twisting of the hog fish took the spear from his hand, and it hit him on the forehead as it swung free. He was knocked unconscious by the blow from the butt of the spear. The fish swam away with the spearhead extending beyond its other side. The diver regained his senses in a moment and surfaced. His companion helped him to their boat where he explained the unusual circumstance. After a few moments, they descended to locate the fish and spear. The long shaft was half visible outside a cave. They pulled and out came the other half, the spearhead driven through the original hog fish and into the brain of another, smaller hog fish. The divers figured that in his maddened fury the first fish had sailed into the cave and dashed against the brain of the other fish. Together they died.

Spears, and later sling weapons, are best for beginners. Their penetrating power is limited but they are still weapons, and all weapons are dangerous. Treat them like rifles. Don't point them at people. Try them on fish—and only when you have a purpose for the fish.

SPRING-POWERED GUNS

Italians were responsible for the development of the Cressi spring-powered guns, which are widely used in this country. Their purpose: to shoot larger fish like the black sea bass, sheepshead, rock fish, sharks, rays, barracudas, ling cod, and others. This gun is primarily a long tube, the center of which is hollow, permitting a coiled spring to be compressed in it when the steel shaft, the spear, is pressed down against the spring. The gun is cocked when the spring is compressed. A steel head at the spear's point does the deadly work, powered by the uncoiling of the steel spring, which propels the spear through the entire length of the hollow shaft, thus keeping the spear on target. The gun is aimed along the length of the hollow shaft just as one aims a rifle. A revolver handle with trigger mechanism is located at the center of the gun. The prone, sitting, standing, or swimming position are all possible with this versatile and powerful gun. The one disadvantage is that the power from a given gun cannot be varied. The diver must own three or four different spring-powered guns in order to hunt for various game. The smaller gun is no more suited for shark than the largest is for grunt.

The choice of gun is again up to the hunter. To really appreciate the difference in weapons, divers should try all types and makes before settling on a favorite. The sport is not unlike game hunting. Jungle, field, mountain, and open range hunters all have their preference of guns, calibers, sights, scopes, weight, and feel. The underwater hunter goes through the same selection of weapons. They have wide variety, again depending upon the game. And after all, one can estimate what game will be hunted. The Mako shark is not usually found in shallow waters any more than the marlin, tuna, or the chinook salmon. Conversely, the moray eel, snapper family, jack, pompano, and the barracuda are shallow-water fish, seldom venturing into really deep waters. Therefore, the hunter usually knows what he will hunt before entering the water and can arm himself accordingly.

The serious spearfisherman will have more than one gun handy. In his floating unit he might have a minor arsenal, capable of taking anything from an eight hundred-pound jewfish to a three-pound grouper. He and his companions are armed to the teeth for any showdown, and it's the foolish diver who spears a fish much larger than his weapon can safely handle.

An underwater joker in the Florida Keys leveled a small spring gun at an enormous sting ray one morning. He had the gun rigged with quarter-inch line. What he hoped to get with the super shark line and a toy gun no one has ever figured out. But later that afternoon, when his two tanks of air gave out, he found himself two miles from where he had speared the ray. He had been towed that distance and was lucky to be in open water, or the ray might have swiped him against one of the many sharp coral reefs, easily tearing him into shreds. The joker abandoned his lead belt, ditched his lung harness and dragged it back to his boat. A less composed man or weaker swimmer might never have returned from such foolishness.

RUBBER-POWERED GUNS

Again the Europeans gained an early foothold in this field. The French were responsible for one of the early rubber-powered models that became very popular in the United States about ten years ago, the single and dual live rubber-powered Arbalete gun, which is today still one of the top-rated guns. American versions of this gun have since come on the market.

These guns are shaped and fired like rifles. Instead of a stock, however, there is a triggered pistol grip, which propels a steel-pointed spear with a detachable screw-head. The power that sends the shaft on its mission is provided by a single or dual set of powerful rubber bands that are attached to the front of the gun. The diver pulls the rubbers back with both hands or feet, depending on how the gun is designed. Notches at various points on the spear receive the rubber-bands, which can thus be set for varying velocities. Dual sets of bands on the larger rubber-powered guns can cope with blue and sand sharks, barracudas, moray eels, giant groupers, and sting rays.

Rubber-powered guns are also made in junior sizes and in models resembling revolvers. These are meant for smaller fish. Most of these guns, both large and small, are simple to handle and efficient, but in order to get maximum penetration they must be aimed at the fish from within six feet or less, depending upon the gun. When the spear has been released, many of the current guns will float, pistol grip up. A fish line usually attaches the spear to the gun proper, although some spearmen prefer not to use a line. Others attach to the spear a strong quarter-inch line that is rigged to a floating boat or surfboard. This rig is for larger fish who will easily tire fighting the boat. A hunter can then get in another shot with another spear as the fish swims about.

In open waters the fully extended prone position is most efficient. Fish in these open waters can easily out-distance swimmers, therefore the prone position gets the diver closer to the fish than other positions. In coral, rock, and kelp areas, all positions are used, and the gun is aimed while sighting down the barrel, or simply extended at arms length, and fired.

A novice spearman had an interesting turn in the Bahamas. He was spearing with his first Arbalete. It was a small model, but he was using an oversized spear that extended about twelve inches beyond the muzzle. In relatively shallow water he impaled a small red snapper of not more than 1½ pounds. He turned around to surface when he came face to face with a sand shark—not long, not short. Not knowing what to do when the shark rushed him, and not knowing that the shark was after the fish, not him, he pushed the snapper, spearpoint, Arbalete, and all, as hard as he could directly into the open jaw of the shark. The shark clamped down hard on the steel shaft, but the point had already gone a foot down his throat, tearing as it went. The diver jerked the gun back, pulling flesh and blood from the sand shark—but not the snapper. The shark took the 1½-pounder, turned his high caudal fin up and fled like a frightened rooster.

Controversy between partisans of the spring and rubber-powered guns has often arisen. Each gun has its advantages and disadvantages. Most rubber guns have safety levers like their land counterparts. Some contend the one-hand-operated spring guns are better than the two-handed rubber guns for the resistance of water is lessened by the smooth lines of the spring gun. But the pros and cons of both guns will have to be weighed by the individual.

COMPRESSED-AIR GUNS

In all big-game hunting there are the big-game guns. A .300 and .375 H&H Magnum or the .348 Winchester are better for elk than the .30/30 Remington. That's a known fact. Graduate into the bigger game and there is a wide selection of guns available.

In the underwater the compressed-air weapons are the big-game guns. They generate penetrating power with a charge of captured air that is fierce. In fact, they created such disturbances in France and Italy, two of the earliest sites of underwater sport, that authorities have barred their use there.

These guns are monsters. Some carry enormous cylinders of air that provide as many as forty "shots" of air. Others are operated by inserting a single cartridge of carbon dioxide similar to the ones used by flyers on their "Mae Wests" during World War II. Each year they get more terrifying. Some guns on the market—and others that are products of home workshops—are capable of killing anything that swims. If a whale were spotted by some underwater extremists carrying their super guns, they would probably attack it without hesitation.

Compressed-air guns scare hell out of fish. The escaping gas bubbles out after the spear like a small waterfall. Fish for miles around hear the racket. Some come to investigate, but others head in the opposite direction. At times, loosing a blast of air at a curious shark will return him to the deeps; but at other times, when the bubbles have cleared away, the diver may be looking down the throat of a particularly angry shark.

With the cartridge-type gun, each shot must be set individually. The cartridge is inserted, fired, and replaced for another shot. With the multi-shot cylinders, unless a waterproofed gauge is attached, there is no telling when the gun is out of compressed air. Sometimes, when the need is great, the diver pulls the trigger and is again looking down the angry maw of a big one. He can always send the gun and all down the fish's throat, turn heels, and swim for cover.

As we become immune to disease, and diseases become immune to penicillin, so some fish get "immune" to compressed-air guns. Grouper, who are creatures of habit, are also observant fish. Off a reef in Bermuda, one spear fisherman saw several grouper basking in the bubbles of his discharged gun. This phenomenon happened too often to be dismissed lightly. He inquired of a master diver and learned what deep-sea divers have known for years. Most fish have parasites on their bodies, and the escaping air, carrying oxygen, offers refuge for the fish that swims into the bubbles. The oxygen kills the parasites for they cannot stand such quantities of pure oxygen. Not bad reasoning for the grouper.

Two divers equipped with guns can easily kill the voracious tiger sharks, oversize jewfish that tip the scales at almost half a ton, or giant manta rays. And hunters everywhere are doing just that. To prove what? Perhaps that guns can be made to shoot the biggest and the deadliest of sea monsters.

Be careful of these high-caliber guns of the underseas. Don't tamper with them unless you know what you're doing. And above all, don't try to build one unless you surely know what you're doing. Eventually, there might be a curb on this menacing weapon. In the hands of experts, it's just another effective weapon. But these guns are available to anyone with the purchase price, and that's the danger that will eventually bring about restraints.

POWER HEADS AND OTHER POWERED GUNS

Bullets can be used underwater in waterproofed rifles. Bullets are also used at the end of the spearhead, set to fire on impact, much like the dum-dum bullets used during World War I. These are called power heads and they began to see light in home workshops, probably in California. After the bullet is fired, the harpoon is driven deeper into the fish. But accidental impact will fire the cartridge, too. A careless solid impact might reverse the forward drive of the shaft, with the explosion backing into the gun. Improper design in home workshops makes this a weapon of destruction.

From Australia comes word that black powder bullets are used with stock rifles that shoot stainless steel shafts effectively to about thirty-six feet. This gun stock for underwater is not new. Otis Barton, co-scientist with William Beebe in their amazing deep water descents in steel spheres, developed an underwater rifle whose explosion stunned fish. He took a Civil War vintage gun and modified it. It was not as effective as he wanted it. The parts corroded in salt water.

Guns are meant for destruction. To treat them lightly is an error. To relax on the recognized safety rules, whether land or underwater guns, is a mistake. Use them, maintain them, and above all, be careful with them. Most of them can just as easily kill your companion as they will your fish.

8

A *New Approach to Angling*

Why do men fish? They seem to be motivated by three basic reasons, and these reasons are as applicable to spearfishing as to any other form. Men fish: (1) for pure sport; (2) for the thrill of the hunt; and (3) for food. Whatever the reason, spearfishing, as the latest addition to popular fishing, has an appeal and a place for all enthusiasts, and then some.

Spearfishing comes down to this: Who can outwit whom? Can man's presumably better brain make up for the obviously superior speed, agility, and motivation of the fish? When man knows his equipment, the fish, and the water well enough, the answer is yes—at least it is often enough to make spearfishing a sport and not a major twentieth-century frustration.

As in all sports in which a living creature is being deprived of life, one thing must be kept in mind—killing for the lust of killing is both objectionable and wrong. Needless slaughter of fish, as of chickens, pigs, cattle, and sheep, cannot be tolerated, and we must be on guard to avoid this at any cost, keeping conservation a primary consideration.

Spearing fish for food, of course, is understandable, and so is the spearing of sporting game fish. There are, however, certain limitations—the self-respecting spearman does not spear hundreds of pounds of eating fish and leave them to rot. Neither does he spear small, inedible tropical fish that are remarkable for their beauty but no great shakes as targets.

Some spearfishermen who have turned their attentions to "looking" reported recently, "It's more fun to watch those crazy fish underwater than to chase them." This interest in watching instead of spearing is, in itself, a conservation factor. As one man said, "I used up three bottles of air watching a conch drag his shell home along the bottom. It was more fun than spearing fish, and next time I'm taking a beach chair down, just to sit and watch."

UNDERSTANDING THE FISH

Not all fish interest the spear fisherman. Where the scientist might be content to observe a rare species of tropical fish, the sportsman seeks out the more dangerous varieties, such as sharks and barracudas, or the more tasty specimens, as the snappers and lobsters. No matter what the motive is, knowing more about the fish you seek is important.

What do we know about fish? For years, their mating, dietary, and living habits have been studied and noted by ichthyologists and amateur fish watchers. Yet it is amazing how little our scientists really know about fish, as compared to other creatures. Why? Perhaps it is because fish live in a world of their own, until recently impenetrable to most of us. It is a world known to man, yet out of reach. When we pull a fish out of water—into our world—at the end of a line, either the fish is dead, or it soon will die of suffocation. Not a very good subject for study.

Of course, dissecting a fish tells us something about it. Watching a fish's habits in an aquarium can bring some information. We can drop a camera into the ocean deeps at the end of a cable to make pictures automatically at designated intervals. The film may reveal rare or unknown fish caught in the lens' angle of view. But all these sources are dreadfully limited.

A woman best learns about children by being a parent. A child learns about puppies by owning one. A student of journalism takes a job as a cub reporter to learn the newspaper business. And so it must be with someone who wants to know fish.

Film studies have been made of the worker ant, who burrows and establishes his castle in twenty feet of earth. The lion and the lioness have been observed with telephoto lenses so that their most intimate secrets are a matter of film record. The giant condor, isolated atop the highest mountain, cannot hide its habits from the prying eyes of man. Lizards of the desert and jungles, elephants of Africa and India, the giant polar bears of the Arctic, who blend themselves to the white wastes, and the shy, little, working beavers—none hide their secrets from us. They, however, live in accessible areas where, with binoculars and cameras, our scientists and naturalists can visit them. It is sometimes hazardous, but at least they are accessible and their lives are not a secret for long.

Free diving with artificial breathing devices has done more for the ichthyologist in his quest for knowledge of inhabitants of the sea than any other single item. In recent years the hidden why's, which only continued undersea study can reveal, have been researched. Studies of living fish have been made under natural surroundings. Depth barriers to areas of mass undersea gowth have been conquered. Scientists have lingered for hours at the base of reefs—a feat possible ten years ago only with heavy diving dress.

Spearing isn't just unleashing a steel shaft at a fish swimming by. It requires more knowledge. The smart spearman will go down to the bottom of the sea where he intends to fish, and just sit there for hours. He'll learn more about fish life by sitting and observing than he'll learn by changing targets without purpose.

How do you get near a fish? Not usually by engaging it in a race. Man, according to a *Life* article, can swim neck and neck with the beaver, polar bear, loon, and eel. Man can beat the shrimp. But man is easily outdistanced by the sailfish, tuna, tarpon, flying fish, trout, dolphin, finback, whale, leatherback turtle, and even the penguin.

By far, the easiest way is to let the fish come to you. Skin divers don't have as much time to wait around for the fish as lung divers. But even while skin diving, if the spearmen will descend several times to the rock, coral, or kelp where the fish is lurking, he will find the fish more inquisitive with each dive. On a fourth or sixth dive, the fish will usually make himself vulnerable.

Lung divers can afford to be patient. They can sit on a rock and just relax. The fish will do the rest. Edible fish will soon become inquisitive and swim close enough to be speared. (This may not be the most sportsmanlike way to stalk a fish, since the fish make excellent targets of themselves.)

All fish are constantly alert. They must be to survive in a sea where to be quick and strong means to survive. The small are prey to the larger, and the larger are prey to the predators. Life below the waters is a vicious circle of eat or be eaten. So fish become alert through natural inclination and a quick motion or an unexpected move will make the fish vanish as quickly as cake and soda pop at a child's birthday party.

This alert awareness of fish raises the classic question—do they have ears?

Until a better theory is evolved, we assume that fish receive vibrations through the ultra-sensitive membranes, the "lateral lines," that extend from the gills to the tail on either side of the body. Since in most fish the organ of sight is weak, they strongly depend upon sound vibrations that are caught by their lateral lines (which are distinguished by a slight modification and color in the scaling). The lateral line is supposed to direct the fish to food, away from obstacles in the water, and to warn them of approaching danger.

Sound waves travel swiftly underwater since there is little hindrance. Sound cannot bounce back until it strikes an object, and these sound vibrations are felt by fish in the area. Sometimes that area is several miles in length, depending upon the origin of the sound.

A scream or the striking of metal or stone objects underwater may well save a life. Loud noise has been seen to have a measurable effect, especially on sharks. When pitted against a shark and there is no other alternative, try yelling madly and/or striking objects together. At the same time, advance toward the shark. If that's the last measure, nothing can be lost, and the mad scramble may scare him off.

Bottom fishing near coral heads, rocks, caves, or rocky ledges requires extreme silence. Try to drift into the scene with the underwater currents, remaining as motionless as possible. This prevents startling the fish; you will, at times, take him off guard—and that's the moment to shoot. But by far, the most important point of bottom hunting is to be near the bottom. A swimmer who hopes to spot his prey from the surface alone will usually come home without fish. Closer inspection of coral reefs and tall-growing kelp beds will reveal a honeycomb of shelters, each a crafty hiding place for the naturally camouflaged fish. Spotting them from ten to twenty feet, at less than perfect visibility, is next to impossible.

Open-water spearfishing is a hazard. High-powered guns are necessary as shooting distances are longer. Oftentimes, the game fish are feeding on the bottom in a sparsely planted area. A cautious, well-timed dive will often bring the spearman over the fish.

Most fish in open water will outdistance a diver. When a spearman finds himself left behind by a grouper darting from coral head to coral head, or by a snapper heading out to deeper and less vegetated water, a smart underwater man will admit he's licked.

Other game fish, as the barracuda, dolphin, and tuna, feed near the surface, and generally if it's the larger fish you're after, they can almost be found swimming into your gun. Expert shooting is necessary in deeper waters, for a wounded fish can make off with your spear and gun unless they are anchored to a floating buoy, a rubber boat, or an inner tube. The floating object will soon tire out the fish, and it, together with your gun, can later be retrieved.

BARRACUDAS

This is the fish causing most anxiety among tropical water swimmers and divers. Study their habits, and you'll learn to respect these agile, alert swimmers. But the more you learn of the 'cuda the more you'll learn to relax while in the water with them.

A speared, bleeding fish will often bring a barracuda to the scene. The last flutters of the fish's fins will alert the 'cuda from long distances, and it will come to survey your scene from ten to thirty feet away. It's usually after the fish on your spear—not you. Offer the fish to the barracuda and it will probably make a pass for it. In a powerful spurt, the 'cuda will take the fish from your extended spear and be off with it before you realize it's gone. That's the end of friend barracuda. It's feasted, and couldn't be less interested in you unless you have another fish to offer.

Most divers have a sixth sense about themselves in warmer waters. Invariably, they seem to know when a barracuda is watching. When that feeling comes, turn your head. Usually there's a 'cuda not a dozen feet behind and above you, opening and closing its mouth with slow rhythmic motion, showing the keen pointed teeth. But if it hasn't attacked before now—relax. If you just want to be left alone, don't show fear and it will do just that. If, however, you're fishing for barracudas, then entice him to you by slowly swimming toward him in steady, definite strokes. Have a powerful spear cocked and ready to shoot him through the gills, the eye, or the brain (just behind the eyes). Try to swim toward him from below. A barracuda may attack a man if at even level or below him, particularly when a spear-fisherman enters or leaves a boat. Get close.

If you can maneuver the barracuda into a shot from less than three feet, do it. A CO_2 gun, a powerhead, a double elastic, or a spring gun will kill a barracuda. Some swimmers still use the simple Hawaiian sling just as effectively. After spearing a 'cuda, stay clear of him. He'll strike wildly if wounded and will then swim away.

The barracuda has been described as looking like a pirate. It does. Its large pointed teeth are menacing. The fish is pike-like in appearance, with a long streamlined silver and blue body. The Gulf of Mexico barracudas are often spotted, with dark bars on the upper portion of their bodies. Their bodies are always well filled out. A skinny looking 'cuda is not often observed; they eat well.

They spawn during the summer months and drop anywhere from fifty thousand to less than five hundred thousand eggs, depending upon the size and age of the female. The great barracuda reaches ten feet, but the average size of the Atlantic species is from two to five feet. The Pacific barracuda is smaller, weighing about ten pounds.

It's peculiar how a barracuda is feared by most fish, yet allowed to mix freely with them at times. It will chase a school of jack until it gorges itself. Then it will lie peacefully among the remaining school without molesting them. Strange companions, they.

Underwater adventurers have tried to tame barracuda.

One succeeded in feeding a 'cuda anchovies from a can daily —but the bait was at the end of a pole. In time, he hoped to feed the 'cuda out of his hand. To date there is no report as to whether this experiment has succeeded—or whether the diver has lost an arm. I personally would not trust a barracuda closer than the point of my spear.

They are unpredictable. They have been known to attack anything that flashes in the water. Swimmers with bright daylight-fluorescent trunks are particularly likely prey. 'Cudas may well attack a white-fleshed bather and leave the sun-tanned one alone.

Habitat of barracudas: wherever there are fish on which they can feed in tropical waters. They are a migratory fish that trail schools of younger fish around shallow waters, and barracudas are seen in groups as well as hunting alone.

MORAY EELS

Another denizen of the deep worthy of consideration is the multi-colored moray eel. The moray deserves no sympathy for he's a dirty fighter and a miserable, slimy fellow to meet in the dark of his rocky hole. His meat is inedible; he has a perpetual sneer, even worse and certainly more ugly than the barracuda. He's the black sheep of the underwater Who's Who, and no kind word has ever been written about him.

His sneaky mien makes his natural habitat where lobsters dwell understandable, and consequently, spearmen who do not know his ways will soon become familiar with them when hunting lobster. A treacherous adversary, the moray slinks his serpentine body from his hole to challenge the prospective lobster hunter. Sometimes the eel will retreat deeper into his hole. More often than not, however, he will stand his ground, ready to attack with his strong jaws and formidable teeth, able to inflict serious wounds.

They are found in all warm waters of the Western Hemisphere, and some species range from the South Pacific to the Mediterranean. Their scaleless bodies, lacking dorsal and pectoral fins, have been known to reach eight feet in length. Propelled by the swaying of their bodies, the morays are content to remain in their immediate home areas, being notorious creatures of habit.

One California report identified a diver who put his hand into the mouth of a moray, just as lion trainers often do with their favorite tame lion. In the case of the moray, the action was stupid. Lions who have been tamed can be trusted by those who understand them, but a moray eel is, by temperament and disposition, mean and aggressive. They should never, under any circumstance, be trusted.

When speared, they will tear themselves to shreds trying to dislodge the spear. They twist up on the shaft, sometimes bending it like a pretzel. One Florida diver puts them into a canvas bag and ties the end. Another presses a second spear beside the one pentrating the moray and applies pressure to hold the eel. He then surfaces, careful to avoid the menacing jaws. Still another diver will not spear a moray unless the line attached to the spear is firmly knotted to his boat. A companion then pulls in the eel and knocks it senseless with a baseball bat before he dares boat him. All this unsympathetic punishment from experienced divers proves that the moray eel is not a companionable fish.

GROUPERS

The groupers are a large family of fish whose dominant characteristic is a continuous dorsal fin that spans most of its back. They are all colors of the rainbow, depending upon the species. The different varieties, from the black and nassau grouper to the yellowtail, brown-tail, rock grouper, red grouper, and many others, are found in waters stretching from Boston to Brazil.

Groupers are a wary lot. They camouflage themselves among coral or rocks. They disappear quickly into their holes, which sometimes makes it necessary to stalk them through other entrances. These fish are creatures of habit, remaining around their eating grounds and straying very little during their entire lifetime. Busy with other projects, one can often watch groupers not six feet away, they are so inquisitive, often coming directly in sight to see what's happening. Their curiosity makes them vulnerable to a spear.

But unless the spear hits true the first time they will flutter back into their holes. That's when the struggle begins. This family of fish expand their dorsal fins and are almost immovable when they have retreated into their lairs. They have been known to recover from spear wounds that have almost pierced vital spots. Some have carried spears around with them while swimming. Pulling on the spear won't budge them. Another and another spear shot into them may do the trick, if one hits true. If unable to spear them again while in the protection of their hole, a bit of trickery may work. Dangle a dead fish or a piece of conch in front of them. They will relax momentarily to reach the delicacy. At that instant, pull on the line or spear.

One group of four divers off Curaçao speared a small jewfish, another of the grouper family, with eleven spears—their entire supply. The fish was still lodged under a deep ledge, unwilling to come out or give up. No amount of pulling could dislodge him. One of the enterprising divers, intent on getting his jewfish, went ashore and returned with a sledge hammer. He pounded away at the coral until he cleared the overhead covering of the ledge. The fish swam out excitedly, but clinging to spears and lines were three spearmen. They boated the seventy-pound fish—a relatively simple job in open water.

SHARKS

Sharks are dangerous. There is no doubt about it. There has been much speculation by shark experts; some say sharks are playful and inquisitive, others say they are aggressive. All are correct. Depending upon his mood, a shark can be any of these. But the word to accept is that of the man who has met sharks face to face in the shark's own back yard. A diver who has been knocked ten feet through the water by the caudal fin of an oncoming shark rushing past him with the speed of an express train is a better authority than an angler who has been fighting and boating sharks with rod and reel even for a generation. The diver has almost felt the hot breath of the shark down his back. One error, and an arm or a head could be missing, and the diver knows it.

The captive sharks in the tourist attractions along the Florida and California coasts are known to be docile, and almost as friendly as goldfish. As long as they get their meals on time, why should they care about hurting anyone?

Even the most audacious experts agree that sharks in open water can be curious, circling up to divers to get a close look at the operation. Known aggressors, like the blue, the white, and the mako shark, barrel-roll along and continue on their way when food is plentiful. The same sharks, when fish dinners are scarce, may spin along with an open mouth, ready to fill it with an arm or a leg or half a torso.

In deep waters, persons on wrecked ships and planes have been known to be victims of shark. In such deeps, food and fish are scarce, and the same shark that will not attack diver or bather in near-shore waters will savagely attack a man far at sea in his crazed desire for food. The empty stomach makes the difference.

A wide variety of sharks are found in waters along both coasts, the Gulf of Mexico, throughout the Caribbean, and in most oceans of the world. Bahama waters are especially full of treacherous sharks. Warm waters and ample feeding grounds make this area ideal for them.

Once, two divers were spearfishing off the island of May-aguana, but somehow they became separated. Scattered mutli-colored coral heads, furrowed brain coral, purple sea fans, and a myriad of tropical fish make it quite simple to become engrossed in the wonders of tropical waters. One diver, on his sixth dive, had just speared a hog fish. Blood colored the blue waters. He was surfacing from about twenty feet when his ascent was blocked by two blue sharks, easily identified by their small anal and second dorsal fins. Their teeth were erect, like chopping blocks. They were on the prowl, and each was easily ten feet long. This was his first shark encounter, and to a fledgling, two ten-foot blues suddenly blocking his ascent seemed unhealthy. He tried to talk himself out of panicking.

He looked for his friend. No friend. He was alone in fifteen feet of water with a dead hog fish and two very live blue shark, both intent on getting fed. But the diver didn't know they were after the fish. He thought they were after his scalp.

In typical shark fashion they circled, closing in with each sweep. The diver backed up against the coral head which towered five feet above him. The coral scraped his shoulders. Blood oozed from the wounds. This new menace added to the sharks' greed. He hung onto his speared hog fish relentlessly. The circle had tightened to a point where the blues were meeting head and tail. He lifted his spearless gun to fend off the shark in a last determined effort of defense when a swoosh of air bubbles appeared on the scene preceded by a blunt steel shaft. His companion, with a compressed-air gun, had come upon the desperate scene from atop the coral head. The friend released the spear at the nearest shark, and followed it with two successive blasts of bubbles, scaring the fish. One blue, with a steel shaft through his gills, turned and fled into the deeper water with the other in hot pursuit.

These and thousands of other encounters with danger underwater only tend to repeat the warning: *Never dive alone.* Stay constantly alert, keeping your companion in view.

Most divers would rather not face a shark in any water. But if, unexpectedly, the battle must be joined, it's best to know how. How do you fight a shark?

First by your wits. Then by strength and courage.

If the diver has a lung and a sharp pointed spear, not even necessarily a heavy duty shark-killing spear, he is in an excellent position to get the better of any shark. Mr. Shark will probably announce his presence by circling around the diver. This gives the diver time to survey his locale. If there's a surface boat handy, make for it gradually. If not, head for a reef or rock that will give protection from the rear. If no shelter is handy, remain in open water and keep facing the shark as he circles.

The circling will tighten. When the shark gets uncomfortably close and you see he means business, jab—don't shoot—with the spear. If you have a heavy weapon—spring or rubber-powered, or one that shoots steel shafts with CO_2 gas—aim for the gills, the eyes, or the brain. If the spear is lightweight, jab, and jab hard, at the snout. That's a very sensitive spot, and sharks do not like the jabbing. One good jab will usually scare him off unless he's extremely hungry. If he persists and the spear is too light for him, head for shore or for your boat. Don't, under any circumstances, turn your back on him.

If a shark appears on the scene while you are skin diving, the best defense is distance. Head for shore or for your boat, and do it quietly. Keep the shark in full view. If diving in rocky areas, try hiding or losing the shark among the vegetation and rocks. Sharks have poor eyesight but can sense direction if the water is being thrashed wildly.

Keep your legs away from the shark's mouth. He'll always attack dangling legs as when the diver breaks for air. At close range use a camera case as a weapon, They are marvelously effective on the snout. If no case is handy, try a double stiff arm or a kick in the face. One of these maneuvers will normally scare the shark away.

The once prosperous shark oil business has dried up, but there is a good demand for the tough shark's skin for the making of ladies' shoes and handbags, jewel cases, briefcases, and wallets. The Greenland shark skin is made into warm footgear for the Eskimos. In the Philippines and in Ceylon, the blue shark's fins are exported for shark-fin soup, a gourmet's delicacy.

In Japan the hammerhead shark is eaten with relish, and in many other parts of the Orient, shark meat, looked upon as non-edible in the Western Hemisphere, is a regular part of the diet. For years, housewives of the Pacific islanders have been using the tough dermal denticles on the shark's skin, for it makes excellent pot scrapers. They last a lifetime and they don't rust. Another wide-spread use for the entire shark is for fertilizer.

In their element, sharks are kings, unapproachable by most fish that swim. They do not fraternize and do not often show acts of kindness to anything that swims. Taken out of their watery kingdom, to be sure, they can be turned into a list of commercial by-products. Here, we control their destinies. But while they still swim, the word is caution. Do not trust them.

Whale shark. The largest fish in the sea is the giant whale shark, weiging upward of twenty-five thousand pounds and measuring up to sixty feet. They are a harmless shark whose diet consists chiefly of small fish and vegetation, which are sifted through a fine set of gill rakers. If a whale shark is accidentally encountered in tropical waters, try to hang on to the dorsal or pectoral fin. Hitch a ride on the largest fish in the sea, and he'll probably never know you're there.

Mako shark. One of the sharks most likely to be encountered in North American waters is the mako, a member of the mackerel shark family. Anglers like the mako because of its unusual stamina, impressively high leaps, and way of splitting steel leaders or tangling the lines when hooked.

Found in tropical waters, they have been caught up to one thousand pounds.

The tail is lunate, equally spaced by the upper and lower lobes of the tail fin.

The mako is a true fighter. Jordan Klein, a Miami underwater camera manufacturer and a noted authority on the underseas, has an entire line of camera cases named after the streamlined mako. He recently illustrated his trademark with a series of hazardous pictures he made of a mako during an encounter, off the Great Bahama Bank. An associate, Pat Henning, speared a twelve-pound snapper that was quickly grabbed by a moray eel lurking in the shadows of the coral head. During the encounter with the twisting moray, a mako entered the scene, bent on taking the struggling eel. The mako struck and the center section of the moray was gone. The mako then grabbed the remaining portion of the eel, which still had the spear attached to it, and headed for Klein and Henning. Klein kicked the shark in the stomach, and the two men quickly got underway to their boat.

Nurse shark. A less aggressive shark than the mako is the nurse, a sluggish, almost lazy, shark usually found feeding in shallows on crab, mussels, and shrimp. They have a noticeably small mouth with very small hard-packed teeth that crunch their food. The dorsals are displaced backward, and the snout is broad and depressed. The nurse is famous in Caribbean and Bahamian waters for being the shark that natives ride. In relatively shallow water, where they can be found feeding, natives jump on their backs, sink their fingers into the fleshy gill slits and twine their feet around the rough skin into a wrestlers' scissor hold. Then they hang on for the ride of their lives.

At times like this the nurse forgets he is naturally sluggish. The nurse's first reaction is to get rid of his jockey. This he does by turning round and round, scraping the back of the rider on the sand or on any rocks or coral in the vicinity. Riders usually drop their grip when the shark heads for deeper waters. If the nurse should turn on the rider, which sometimes happens when the shark is more enraged than embarassed, it's a good idea to have several companions in the water, armed with spears to jab the shark in the head.

Nurse shark grow to ten and even fourteen feet but the usual size is from six to eight feet. More intelligent than many of its cousins, a hooked nurse will remain quietly on the bottom instead of fighting the steel and tearing his mouth or body to pieces. They live longer in captivity than many other sharks, and when captured and towed by a boat they will survive if the tow line is attached to their pectorals. (If towed by the tail for even a quarter of a mile they will drown.)

Hammerhead shark. Another shark commonly seen on both the east and west coast is the hammerhead, a species that has small denticles instead of scales and an unusually shaped head that resembles a battering ram. The eyes are on the forward corners of the ram. This shark's coloring is greyish with a light belly. The upper lobe of the tail is longer than the lower portion, and the caudal peduncle is not keeled as in other species. The hammerhead, whose liver is an excellent source of vitamin *A*, is a migratory fish, a strong swimmer, often showing up in Long Island Sound from their tropical waters during the mid-summer months. They make their way up in the Gulf Stream and continue northward after the stream turns northeast at Cape Hatteras.

In tight battle they are relentless, using their hammer-like heads to batter food fish. Best advice to divers is to let these sharks alone.

Tiger shark. A smaller but equally vicious cousin is the well-named tiger shark. Zane Grey, one of the truly great game fishermen, caught a tiger off Sydney Heads in Australia, weighing 1036 pounds. In 1939 Grey's record was broken in the same area with a catch that weighed 1,382 pounds, according to the International Game Fish Association.

Two Miami diving experts once encountered a tiger in Biscayne Bay. Together, they pumped steel shafts propelled by the force of compressed CO_2 into the shark. After the initial impact, one of the divers backed off to make pictures of his buddy shooting more spears into the tiger. The shark was no match for the blunt edge steel spears.

The tiger, named for the stripes running the length of its back (more pronounced in the younger ones), lives in tropical waters. The Caribbean, and the Bahama, Bermuda, and Florida waters in this hemisphere are the nestling grounds for tiger sharks, which, during the summer months, venture as far north as Cape Cod. These voracious sharks can be identified easily by their tremendous bulk of a head, a short pushed-in snout, and sharp guillotine-like teeth—a sight no diver will ever forget.

Sharks are known to have survived through all geologic ages since the Devonian age, some 350 million years ago. The American Museum of Natural History in New York has on display the restored jawbone of a prehistoric shark (*carcharodon megalodon*) whose open jaws are about six feet high, capable of swallowing several men whole. The jaws look something like those of the present-day "man-eater," the white shark, and the closest living relative of the extinct giant.

Thresher shark. Easily identified by the tremendous sweep of the upper lobe of the tail, which makes up more than half the body at times, are the threshers. Their teeth are weak, not nearly the formidable defense of those of the mako. Their bulk has been known to exceed nine hundred pounds, and a common length is fourteen to sixteen feet. They are not fully mature until at least fourteen feet. Their tail is a useful part of the body. With it they round up schools of fish, coralling them as cowboys and horses corral dogies on the prairies.

Sand shark. These are found in relatively shallow warm water, but sometimes venturing as far north on the Pacific coast as Oregon. Their meat is considered edible by some fishermen. The teeth are short but sharp, set in several rows.

Natives in the pearling waters of the Coral and Timor Seas, and in the Pacific and Indian Oceans, have been known to dive in shark-infested waters, shooing the sharks away. The less hungry shark can be shooed by pearlers or anyone, but even the fearless pearlers, too, have lost arms and legs when a shark's appetite is running high.

Blue shark. Insatiable fish, capable of mean destruction to both man and fish, they are scavengers that follow ships for miles and miles, hoping for a garbage hand-out. Whalers are very familiar with the blues, which seem to show up by the score when a whale has been killed. The sharks make passes at the whale like peeling jets, chomping a mouthful of blubber with each sweep. Hundreds of pounds of whale have vanished before the whalers can complete their job of hauling the carcass into the whaleship.

Blues are streamlined marauders, measuring eighteen

feet and longer. They have an exceptionally long pectoral fin and a long upper lobe. They often attack in pairs, and when the blood of killed fish is spreading through the water, they will accumulate in schools. They make speedy manuevers, an important reason why spearmen should hunt in pairs in tropical blue shark waters.

White shark. The aggressiveness of this monstrous shark has earned him the name of "man-eater." Actually, many more than the white shark are man eaters but the scary size, the large triangular teeth, the long powerful lunate tail fin, and the large pectorals make the white shark specially feared by men of the sea. Fifteen and twenty foot white sharks are not uncommon. Seven thousand pound monsters, while not common, have been hooked.

There is no known record of a white shark being speared. If underwater men encounter a white, the advisable action is to head for shore or for the nearest protection. Several powerful CO_2 guns might stop him with hits in vulnerable spots, but this aggressive action against one of the more powerful fish in the seas is not recommended.

The white is found in tropical waters, but occasionally, during the summertime, they venture as far north as Newfoundland.

LOBSTERS

Lobsters, one of the more popular delicacies of the seas, are taken by spear, claw hook, by gloved hand, and by traps. During the legal fishing season, the commercial fisherman traps lobsters in wire baskets, weighted to keep them on the bottom. The claw is a hook that clamps over the lobsters middle, thereby taking him alive. The skin diver occasionally uses the claw, but it is more frequently used by boat fishermen using glass bottom buckets to spot the lobster in their rocky crevices.

Skin divers use gloved hands and many varieties of spears to catch their lobsters. The gloved underwater men seek them out in the rocks and ledges. They reach in and drag them out. Barbed feelers or claws, depending on the species and the waters, plus the bony sharp tail ridges, are the only weapons these crustaceans have. Heavy gloves protect the diver sufficiently. But one enemy of the diver who puts his hands into dark holes and under deep ledges is the voracious moray eel. A known habit of this dreaded fish is his ability to cling tenaciously to his prey. Free-air skin divers are far more vulnerable than lung divers, who at least have an opportunity to fight back, with the advantage of a continued air supply.

In areas where lobster spearing is not restricted, divers locate them by looking for the tell-tale protruding feelers. The prone shot is best. Sometimes the diver must hold to a piece of coral, or enter a cave, or crawl under wrecks or rock ledges where they like to live. A spear though the head will result in lobster for dinner. (The tail is the edible portion, and in the species that have claws, the meat within them is also edible.)

Lobster's tails propel them in flight, and their hard shell, claws, and spiny back give protection against enemies. Usually they live and spawn in shallow water. In some waters laws limit the size, length, and season when lobster may be taken. Conservation measures in most lobster grounds prohibit the taking of lobster during spawning season. Some local laws even identify the weapon or method by which lobster may be caught. Certain species grow to thirty pounds or more, although the meat on these old lobsters is considerably tougher.

ABALONES

This member of the mollusk family is peculiar to the Pacific coast of Mexico and California. The abalone is a noted delicacy when properly prepared and is considered a rare dinner treat in areas away from its habitat.

The abalone's physical make-up consists of a half shell, attaching and holding itself to rock with a muscular foot. The shell successfully protects it against most prey.

Several varieties are common to west coast areas, notably being identified by color, for example, the red, black, pink, and green abalones. The reds grow largest, extending more than twelve inches across the shell. The shell's inner lining is mother-of-pearl and is used for buttons and inlay work.

The abalone camouflages itself perfectly with sea life. Barnacles and seaweeds are often growing on its shell, and there is little contrast to distinguish it from natural ocean bottom. The skin diver uses an iron bar and sometimes the steel blade of a knife to dislodge the abalone from its rock.

THE RAYS

This distant cousin of the shark is normally a shallow-water dwelling fish whose movements are sluggish, indolent, and without emotion. The ray family includes the skates, the tremendous mantas, the sting and whip rays, the electric rays, and the guitar fishes. Most rays are over-developed sharks whose bodies have pancaked, rounding out the pectoral fins into wings that undulate, thus providing their means of movement underwater.

They are generally inactive fish, roaming on the bottom and burrowing themselves in sand. They take in water through spiracles, large breathing holes found behind the eyes. Their means of defense is limited. The weapon of the rays is not the teeth—they don't have giant protruding teeth like the sharks or barracudas. Instead, there are close-packed teeth that act like a pressure plate, capable of applying great pressures to the shell of clams and oysters, the mainstay in their diets.

The sting ray's only real weapon is a saw-edged spine that grows to twelve or more inches, sometimes growing in clusters of two and three. The ray uses the spine as a dagger, relentlessly piercing its prey or enemy with it. The spine does not inject a poison into the system, but it is usually covered with minute sea bacteria, which have an unpleasant effect on people who are stabbed. The whip tail of some other rays is injurious since it is often covered with sharp barnacles, which inflict stinging wounds.

In the Bahamas and in offshore waters of Florida, some intrepid underwater adventurers have taking to riding the tail of sting rays, not unlike the game of snap-the-whip which ice skaters play. These daring men first spear a ray in the fleshy part of the wings. They then cut off the saw-toothed spines and clean off all the barnacles from the tail. A diver holds onto the tail with gloved hands and the ray is released. With powerful sweeps of its wings it forges ahead, carrying the clinging diver in a mad-swirling series of figure eights through the water. The ride is unlike any other experienced.

The power of the brute can easily be felt—he can drag a two hundred pound passenger effortlessly. With its only weapon eliminated, the ray is helpless. It will not attack its rider as a shark might do when one hitches a ride on its back. But the ray's powerful sweeps can easily throw the rider against a coral head or against rocks.

On one such foray in the Bahamas, a rider was enjoying himself so much that he forgot the usual precautions of such spectacular sport. The six-foot ray headed about madly, tearing up and down through some twenty-five feet of water. The rider clung to the tail like a child enjoying his first pony ride, not realizing the danger of the razor sharp coral, which grew everywhere. The instant before being slammed against an extended coral head while sailing through the water in a tremendous burst of speed, the diver suddenly saw before him the jagged coral growth and instinctively released his hold. He fended himself off with his gloved hands, and only glanced off the sharp coral, instead of taking the full impact with his body as the ray had obviously intended.

Spearmen attack sting rays in tropical waters for little reason. They are useless as a food fish, although excellent bait for shark and lobster traps. Some divers cut off the spines for underwater souvenirs. In time, the rays grow another set of spines, directly behind the original set.

The manta ray is erroneously identified as an aggressive fish. Actually it is not, but its bulk, breadth, and enormous mouth have made it very much feared. Mantas grow to be more than twenty feet across the back and have been caught in excess of three thousand pounds. But they are true vegetarians. They are most feared by deep-sea helmet divers since their wings and bulk often tangle the diver's life

bade fish usually avel in schools, and hen they are to-ether they are easy photograph. They ave black stripes ver silvery skin, re-mbling angel fish. he diver, not four et from this group, id not frighten bem.

and Gustav Dalla Valle)

Veteran diver and world adventurer Hans Hass made this picture of his wife sitting on a coral mound several years ago—proving that little fish are not frightened by invading divers.

(Hans Hass—Black Star)

(Left) *Most fish are gracious hosts, and more often than not they cooperate with divers.* (Below) *Divers and an underwater cameraman casually play with two baby octopuses in the deep waters of the Mediterranean. Octopuses, even the largest, are timid and retreating.* (Top, right) *Small fish of the sea make a pattern against the underwater growth that is difficult for the surface artist to capture—unless he discovered the new wealth of the subsurface with canvas and oils.* (Bottom, right) *Turtles and a mixed variety of small fish swim peacefully in the preserve established at this tourist attraction in Florida.*

Shark fighting, at best, is for experts. In the Bahamas four youths—the youngest nine, the eldest fourteen—attacked a sand shark in open water. Veteran skin divers all, these experts with the home-made Hawaiian sling qualify as spearfishermen the way many divers who are much older would like to qualify!

(John Tassos)

The youngsters attacked in pairs and in less than sixty seconds the shark had four steel spears in his gills. Here fourteen-year-old Buck Hall is administering the coup de grace—tearing the shark's gills with a knife.

The sand shark is whipped, dead, and bleeding—beaten in his own haunt by four veterans of the spear in Bahamian waters. Two of the boys pull him to the surface. The shark—five feet, eleven inches long—was longer than any of the four attackers and weighed sixty-nine pounds—more than the weight of three of the boys.

Eager hands help the boys to boat the shark. In 1952 the same four youths were attacked by a white "man-eater" shark, off Hog Island in the Bahamas. One suffered a laceration of the head. The shark was in unusually shallow water but was after a bleeding fish one of the boys had at the end of his spear. The shark got the fish but failed to dampen the spirits of the wounded lad, who was back in the water soon afterwards.

(Top, left) *The sport* *shark riding has limi* *appeal to a select group* *adventurers—like memb* *of a suicide club.* *shark are not rideal* *since some species are a* *aggressive. The nur* *shark, left, is far from* *tame shark but is mo* *prone to the sport th* *most. In Bahama wate* *the author has just taken* *running jump for n* *nurse shark's back while* *was feeding in shallow w* *ter. The author grabb* *for its pectoral fins. (Be* *tom, left) The shark's fi* *reaction is not unlike t* *bucking of a wild Brahm* *bull. It turned over an* *over as the author tried* *apply a wrestler's scisso* *hold on its body. T* *shark is snorting water,* *sign of fear, since shar* *take in water through t* *mouth, retain the oxyge* *and expel the used wate* *through the gills.*

(Professor John F. Storr)

The author finally succeeded in closing the scissors hold and is still hanging o *to the pectoral fins. The remora fish, the nurse shark's pilot, is sucking on th* *shark's belly. Spearmen who were in the water but out of camera range pro* *tected me. A native dinghy hovers nearby in event of emergency.*

*The nurse shark fought like a fiend. It rolled over and over. The author dug his
fingers into its gill slits, which cut its resistance down considerably, since it
couldn't expel water through the stopped-up gills. Eventually it would choke—
but, if it had kept the author under it much longer, he would have too. On the
last roll shown in this picture, it broke his scissors grip.*

(Professor John F. Storr)

*(Top, right) Here the
author is losing his
body scissors hold. He
thought his right leg
would break when it hit
the water with a snap.
But he moved his hands
to the pectoral fins for
a firm grip and turned
the shark over. (Bottom,
right) The author stood
up in the shallow water
and lifted the shark
with him. The nurse
was starry-eyed and
dead tired. Sharks tire
easily but they recover
immediately. The au-
thor's fingers are still
covering the gills, and
the shark is expelling
water through its
mouth. The author
jackknifed away and
the nurse swam into the
deep without looking
back.*

The barnacle-covered steel smokestack of a sunken ship makes an impressive underwater scene for these lung-diving photographers using dual air tanks. The long cylindrical unit in the diver's hand is a waterproofed torpedo, which houses a camera and a self-contained, battery-powered light. Some torpedoes are equipped with electric motors and propellers for towing divers through the water.

(H. Broussard)

Underwater wreckage always presents an eerie sight. Years of exposure to the underwater always covers wreckage with flora, algae, and barnacles. Two lung divers, one equipped with a torpedo camera, nestle comfortably amidst what was once a floating ship.

(Max Brandily—Photo Representatives)

(H. Broussard—Photo Representatives)

(Top, left) *Three lung divers examine and photograph a sunken wreck. The bubbles on the right are coming from the air bottles of the diver at the bottom of the picture. The Dauphin Torpedo contains a 6-volt, 20-ampere battery with sufficient charge for approximately one hour of motion picture filming and also has an electric motor and propeller that will function at one knot per hour for one hour.* (Bottom, right) *A diver wearing a shallow-water helmet in Florida waters examines two cannons, deeply covered with crusted barnacles. The outer waters of the Florida Keys are scattered with cannons and wrecks of old trade and pirate ships.*

(Jordan Klein)

(Carroll Seghers—Black Star

The moray eel is easily one of the ugliest fish of the sea. It is slimy and often battle-scarred, with a fierce-looking mouth and eyes. It will attack a diver who is foolish enough to probe his hand into the darkness of the eel's rocky hole. Then it holds its grip tenaciously, letting up only to improve the grip. Here a Florida skin diver holds off a maddened moray with a steel spearhead through its head. The moray fought ferociously and tangled the spear's line.

The moray, more accustomed to the rocks and darkened holes of coral, is seldom seen in open water. A giant moray more than six feet long was speared in Florida waters with a sling spear or pole gun. The hole in the upper right-hand side of the moray's head shows where the spear penetrated its brain, killing it instantly.

(Jordan Klein)

The barracuda is another of those often misunderstood fish—accused of more aggressive tactics than can be proven. It is not the easiest fish to approach or spear, but when speared, contrary to popular conception, it usually turns and swims the other way. Here a barracuda speared in West Indian waters is in the first stages of maddened agony, opening and closing its mouth in obvious pain.

(Philip Nash and Gustav Dalla Valle)

This barracuda close-up shows a vicious profile with a determined, underslung jaw—sleek and streamlined for fast maneuvering. The 'cuda is easily recognized by irregular black spots in its after section; by silvery sides; by a white bottom; and by a grey, black, or green dorsal. The spear here has penetrated through the gills —a vital spot.

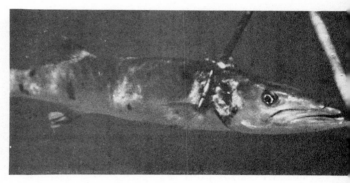

A spear separates the massive jaws of the barracuda for an underwater close-up. Veteran diver Gustav Dalla Valle has a firm grip above the head. 'Cuda travel alone, in groups of two or three; and around wrecks hundreds of barracuda may be seen steeped in layers, one above the other, lying motionless.

(Philip Nash and Gustav Dalla Valle)

(Left) *Spearfishing is popular with people of all ages. I met this nine-year-old youth in the Bahamas—already a veteran of almost four years' diving. He fashioned his spears from beach umbrella rods, inner tubes, and bamboo.*

(John Tassos)

(Top, right) *He chases a parrot fish into a hole on the bottom of the ocean. The "shooter" is ready for action.* (Bottom, right) *Chest deep into the hole the skin diver goes—something not too many grown-ups often do. In twenty seconds or less the lad's eyes will become accustomed to the darkness of the hole and he will be able to see his fish.*

The youngster has just unleashed his spear at the parrot fish and is now coming out of the hole.

The spear can vaguely be seen sticking the parrot fish through the gills —a perfect shot under difficult conditions. The youth is surfacing with a fish that is almost as long as he.

Underwater photography is open to professionals with watertight cases housing Contax or Rolleiflex— or to amateurs with an inexpensive Mako Holiday Brownie camera and case. Skin diver Noah Sarlat spears a lobster in six feet of water off Rose Island in the Bahamas. The picture was taken with a Mako Holiday.

Tropical fish collecting as a hobby, sport, and business has spread rapidly since underwater activity became popular. A skin diver in less than twenty-five feet of water is shown here catching fish with a nylon net amidst the coral formation off the Florida coast.

U.S. Navy Frogmen, in 1955, began extensive underwater reconnaissance surveys which included the checking of navigable channels across the top of Canada. Two divers, wearing cold-resistant rubber suits, are shown descending into the Bering Sea with lifelines tied to their bodies.

(Department of Defense Photo)

H.S.H. Prince Rainier of Monaco, a devoted underwater diver and photographer, has been exploring the Mediterranean Sea for more than seven years. His favorite subsurface sites lie off Corsica, Sardinia, Elba, and the Balearic Islands, although he has visited other areas such as the Canary Islands and Dakar. During his trip to the U.S.A., late in the winter of 1956, he noted in an interview that Florida waters were too cold and that he did not find it opportune to dive. His underwater activities are principally photography and searches for archaeological objects, such as pottery and amphorae from the Roman and Greek eras. In these two pictures he is shown aboard his luxurious yacht, Deo Juvante II, preparing to dive. He wears an Aqua Lung and a rubber shirt.

(Fausto Picedi)

lines, cutting off the surface air supply. A powerful slap from a manta's wing can also disable a boat or scuttle it. Mantas sail through the water with ease, despite their bulk. They seem to skip through tons of water like a nimble Irish lassie hotfooting into a jig.

THE OCTOPUS

This is about the most misunderstood fish of the sea. The octopus, supposedly a man-eater, is actually a timid, retiring, and disinterested mollusk. Its strong beak and the jet black fluid it jettisons into the water when in danger are its two weapons of defense. Furthermore, it can change color at will when angered, frightened, or being chased. Its eight arms, sometimes eaten by the octopus itself in captivity, are useless in open water. They cannot apply tension to their arms or to the suction cups that hold on to prey, except when anchored on a rock, a wreck, or something substantial in the sea. They flounder about helplessly in open water, their arms, attached to a membrane at the base of the body, hanging limply.

They are both cold and warm water mollusks, principally found in the Mediterranean, ranging up to about six to eight feet from tip to tip. In the Atlantic and the Pacific, they have been known to range to fourteen feet. They frequent dark caves, old wrecks, barrels, and discarded boilers. These eight-armed cephalopods eat giant crabs mostly, but the Greeks dangle meat on hooks to lure them from their darkened holes. Another lure that gets them out of their caves is the use of salt, since they are known to be allergic to excessive amounts. For an effective shot, spearmen hunting the octopus must spear them in the brain.

Baby octopus is a rare delicacy in many countries. In Hawaii the tentacles are reversed and cooked. They are then dipped in a Japanese *Miso* sauce made of freshly mashed soy beans, garlic, ginger, and soy sauce.

Greek seamen for generations have tenderized octopus by beating it against the rocks. The skin is reversed, cleaned, and then cut up and marinated in olive oil, wine vinegar, fresh oregano, crushed garlic, and Spanish onion. Another famous Greek recipe for tenderized octopus calls for frying the choice bits in olive oil and eating them as a *mezze* (appetizer) with the national drink, *ouzo*, made from fermented white grapes.

OTHER FISH

Pacific black sea bass, popularly known as jewfish, are monsters. A 410-pounder was speared by a diver from San Diego, who used a powerful gun whose nylon line was attached to a floating paddle board. The bass fought the paddle board instead of the diver, and in three hours, the bass was brought to shore. Anglers who tie into this brute should be prepared for a long battle to the finish. They like to feed in water up to fifty feet deep, free from kelp. Bass steaks are a popular Pacific delicacy.

Other sport fish that test the underwater spearmen are wahoos and dolphins, although both are open-water fish and are rarely speared. The sailfish, another open game fish, is a choice eating fish that seldom meets with spearmen. But one became victim to Art Pinder of Miami, one of the country's outstanding skin divers, who, with a hand-made speargun, established a kill that has not, to date, been duplicated. Other game fish are the cero-mackerel, the albacore, broadbill swordfish, the white and striped marlin, and the amazingly swift tuna.

Among the highly edible non-game fish are the great family of groupers, usually found among rocks and coral; the equally large family of shallow-water snappers; pompanos, mackeral, bonitos, snooks, halibut, blackfish, jacks, the mutton fish, and hundreds of others—all spearable and all eagerly sought by hunters on all coasts.

9

The Sidelines: Special Interest Diving

THE OCEAN IS AS FASCINATING as it is wide and deep. The real sense of that fascination comes, not to the man who casts a line into the water, but to he who tastes its salt and freshness, parts the seaweed to see a startled fish double up a caudal fin and scamper away, or barrels through the water like a porpoise. Fascination comes with diving through multi-colored gorgonia, fanlike and still in calm waters; with diving to the bottom of the ocean to scoop up a handful of soft sand; with inspecting the work of nature underwater—the mountains and valleys and caves alive with fish.

Looking is still the first basic activity of any underwater student. After becoming acquainted with a new world, he may be led to try fish spearing. But bringing fish home to the table is only one of the sidelines. A whole new vista has been opened by the mask and the breathing device. For the daring who want added excitement there is cold water and night diving. For those who do not live near the great oceans there is fresh-water diving. The adventurer may seek sunken wrecks bearing treasures and myth, and encounters with the storied "monsters" who always seem to be guarding the wealth. The shell collector has a new and exciting way of adding to his own treasures, and the tropical fish collector visits the home grounds of the specimens he needs.

Even the artist has found new scenes and landscapes to paint. Two serious artists from Palos Verdes, California, whose specialty is lung diving, compounded special paints and prepared canvasses, and descended into the water to paint their impressions of life beneath the surface. Amid the curious fish, a delightfully polite sort of kibitzer, they leaded down their easels to hold them on the bottom and painted away as long as the air in their lungs lasted.

COLD-WATER DIVING

Stagnant water will freeze at thirty-two degrees F., but moving waters of the sea, rivers, and large lakes do not freeze at any temperature because of the water's constant motion. In the Arctic, surface waters freeze solid, but beaneath the tons of ice is moving water, at "freezing" temperature but still moving.

Who wants to dive in freezing water, one asks, and why? It's another element to conquer. So divers slip into freezing fresh and salt water, chop holes through the ice to see how fish survive, and brave icy winds and numbing temperatures to pursue their sport. It takes perfect health and some bravado to fight freezing weather and water. It also takes specialized equipment.

In all seasons, in waters off the coasts of Canada, Greenland, Iceland, Newfoundland, British Columbia, the northeast and northwest coasts of the United States, in frozen lakes everywhere, men are going down to look at life under winter's cover. How can they survive such cold water?

Two kinds of rubber suits do the trick. The wet suit system capitalizes on the mechanics of body heat. It is made of foam rubber and is worn without any undergarments. Water seeps into the suit and is there lodged between the inner layer of the suit and the skin. The captive water is soon brought to body temperature by the heat normally given off by the body. The warmed water, held there by the porous suit, forms an insulating layer that prevents further heat loss. Simple? Yet it works, in moderately cold water. Best results with wet suits are in waters not colder than about fifty degrees F. Wet suits can be worn with artificial breathing gear or simply with mask and fins. They must fit snugly, otherwise the diver will become water-logged.

The dry suit is completely waterproofed, and in it, a diver can be comfortable for hours. The suit should fit properly, allowing for warm underclothes—long-johns, sweaters, and heavy wool stockings. Rubber mittens, a full face mask, and a hood that covers the entire head except the face complete the ensemble for freezing-water diving.

Rubber suits add to a diver's buoyancy since there is captive air within the suit. That means he will have to readjust his lead weights in order to maintain the correct neutral buoyancy in the water. Another weight added to the lead belt will usually take care of this added buoyancy.

Our bodies must remain at a constant temperature close to 98.6 degrees F. An adipose layer of fat, to a small extent, keeps the body warm. But when large amounts of body heat begin to leave the body, it is a warning to the diver to get out and restore lost heat. When the fingers seem immune to pain, and the feet do not respond to thumping on rocks—that is a serious warning for the diver to leave the water immediately. Limbs can freeze, the entire body can be dangerously chilled, and unless it's restored to normal temperature, death can result. The best way to restore lost heat is to do it gradually, by entering a room whose temperature can be increased by degrees. If a warm room is not available, a bonfire will do almost as well, or preferably two fires with the victim standing or lying between them.

Before the development of rubber suits, it took years of body-punishing training for members of winter swimming clubs to train themselves for cold-water swimming. Such clubs are still active in the Great Lakes and other Middle West lakes and on both the East and West Coasts. People watching winter swim club members taking a dip in the lakes and oceans with snow on the ground thought they were crazy; they still do, even if rubber suits have been added.

Houdini, the famous magician who died in 1926, was an accomplished cold-water swimmer who used the unique ability in one of his acts. On a winter day, he was manacled by hand and leg irons and thrown through a hole chopped in the Lake Erie ice. He removed the restraining irons easily, as usual, but encountered difficulty in finding the hole again. For three and one half minutes, the peak of endurance to which he had trained himself to hold his breath, he sought in vain for the hole. (Swiming in freezing water saps the energy from a diver's body faster than in tropical water, so his ability to hold his breath was indeed amazing.) In desperation, he sought to break through the ice, but it held. But as he clawed at the deadly barrier, he saw air bubbles under the ice—captive air bubbles that had been unable to escape when the water froze. Those accumulated bubbles provide enough air to keep him alive. He swam about for twelve minutes before he found the hole, and when he emerged, no one would believe a mere mortal could hold his breath for twelve minutes, especially in freezing water (which, of course, he had not). His assistants were astonished too; all had given him up for lost.

Cold-water divers have been called upon to perform minor miracles, too. One spirit-dampened young lady lost her engagement ring in Boston Bay, off Marblehead, on a January evening. She called upon two winterized skin divers, who probed the muck and debris of the bay for several hours. Finally, up they came, clutching the ring on a fish line between them. The lady today wears her ring on the same fish line around her neck. She thinks skin divers are wonderful people. She married one.

In descending through a hole in ice, the crucial safety measure is, of course, a lifeline tied securely around the waist of everyone entering the water. A capable assistant, who understands prearranged signals for hauling in if the diver is in trouble, should tend the line.

Though diving into freezing water is not as yet a mass sport, there do seem to be a few thousand divers in the country who practice their sport the year round.

Some do it for a very specific purpose. The U.S. Navy

has a group of divers connected with the Underwater Demolition Team who specialize in cold-water diving. They have been conducting on-the-site reconnaissance surveys of beaching locations and checking navigable channels through seldom-used passages connecting main water arteries in northern Canada and along the north coast of the Alaskan peninsula. These maneuvers are the first steps toward piling up necessary knowledge of territorial defense measures should our country be invaded from this isolated northern sector.

But other non-military cold-water diving is practiced mostly for sport and unusual adventure. It is done privately by individuals and by diving clubs. The gear has been designed largely by the development and research groups of the Navy and is now available to the public. But this specialized diving is a young mans' game, and all of those who practice it know it. It can be uncomfortable. With the wet suit, the first few minutes are cold and mean. The dry suit is immeasurably more comfortable from the outset. Wet or dry suit, breathing becomes more labored in cold water, which easily saps more energy than seventy-two degree water.

The philosophy of cold-water diving was explained rather grimly by a devotee, one who went diving in February in Nova Scotia for the first time. "It's my choice," said he, "and I'm learning to live with it."

NIGHT DIVING

In man's frenetic effort to escape the commonplace, he has reached for everything, including the moon. Underwater diving was uncommon until a few years ago. Now it is the fastest-growing sport in the world. Men have conquered the undersea and have mastered many of its unknowns. Above all, man has learned how to see underwater. And now, the miracle of sight below the surface having been achieved, what does man do? He reverts to underwater darkness. Now that he has discovered how to see underwater, he goes diving at night—when he cannot see anything. Only man can outdo man.

But it takes guts to dive at night. It's an eery feeling. It is walking softly in a "haunted house," walking with quickened pace down the middle of the road on the way home after midnight. Anyone who does that deserves to be scared.

Night diving is all that. Going into the water on a moonless night is like descending into a void; there is no sea floor, no sea surface. Down looks like up and up looks like down. Except for the increasing pressure, there is no way for the diver to know in which direction he is heading. The surface is as black as the bottom. If there is no moon, unless a diver hangs a lantern from the side of his boat, he will not even know which side is up. When the eyes eventually become accustomed to darkness, as to the light inside a cave or in the interior of a sunken ship, rocks and reefs and the silhouette of your boat become apparent. The only light comes from the millions of tiny phosphorescent organisms that twinkle like distant stars. You move slowly and carefully. You feel aware of fish lurking in the darkness, watching your every move. The silence is deafening. You sense the movement of fish, perhaps through the quivering of the water.

Then you light up an underwater flashlight. It could be anything from a three-cell waterproof flashlight to the new Mako sealed-beam developed by Jordan Klein, which works on 110 AC volts from the boat overhead. The beam plays on the rocks and the bottom, striking scampering fish and passing lightly over globehorn and swaying kelp or eel grass. The beam penetrates ten or twenty feet, but as suddenly as the area becomes bright with light it returns to darkness again as the beam sweeps on. Your imagination plays games again. You move the light around swiftly in an attempt to light the complete perimeter about you. It's useless. The beam throws light only in one direction at a time, leaving the rest in blackness.

Some fish are known to feed at night, and divers go spearfishing for them armed with a speargun and a torch. Under such circumstances, it's best to use a gun that can be operated simply and effectively with one hand. A line should be attached to the spear, otherwise a fish might swim away with it.

Some fish are blinded by the light and swim into it. Shrimp are caught with nets at night by shining a lantern on the surface of the water. Lobster can be netted, too. The light will attract and blind them, making them easy prey for a net.

It's best to avoid larger fish since a wounded fish may turn and attack. In the darkness, it's easy to lose direction and coordination, and panic—even for the most experienced divers. All daylight precautions should be doubled for night diving. It's dangerous, at best, to be walking on slippery rocks, diving through heavy kelp, or swimming through coral-infested waters.

Since fish like to feed at night, and more often near the surface, night divers will find ample company on their evening expeditions. Two ardent female skin divers once descended into fifteen feet of water off the Gulf coast near New Orleans. On their backs they carried their net knapsacks for shells and fish specimens. Their mission was to watch the night movement of the sea cucumber and tropical fish. Throughout their time on the bottom they felt that they were not alone in the darkness. Movement around them stirred their imagination. They stayed close to one another. The darkness seemed to close in on them—and always there was movement close behind them. Their torches failed to reveal anything, until finally that strange motion actually touched the back of one of the girls. Her open knapsack had inadvertently caught a small flounder. The little fellow was hopelessly tangled in the net bag, and the skin diver was almost frantic trying to identify the cause of the commotion on her back.

In the darkness, skin divers will realize, it takes curiosity and lots of guts to enter the black waters, beneath whose surface anything can happen.

FRESH-WATER DIVING

The waters of the trout, the gar and dogfish, the lake and river bass, the fighting salmon, and all the other fresh-water fish are as important to some divers as the waters of the ocean fish. Those who live inland, away from the East and West and Gulf Coasts, who infrequently have opportunity to visit the oceans, have made inland water fishing their own private sport.

Within our borders are some mighty lakes and rivers. The third longest river in the world is the Mississippi-Missouri, and Lake Superior is the largest lake in the world, while its neighboring Lake Huron and Lake Michigan are fourth and fifth largest, respectively. Sprinkled generously throughout the country, in addition to these mighty fresh-water bodies, are thousands of smaller lakes and rivers and their tributaries. Many of these waters have attracted underwater fans.

Many more will follow. There is no count of the number of such fans, but activity has been reported in many states.

How good is fresh-water diving? Can one see as clearly in fresh water as in the ocean? What can you spear? What is there to see?

The lure of fresh water is not unlike that of ocean underwater activity. It requires the same equipment and involves similar risks, excitement, and adventures. Club activity and individual spearfishing reports are coming in from the inland water areas more and more heavily.

Lake Tahoe in Nevada has seen a tremendous increase in underwater activity. Clear waters there, and in Lakes Donner and Topaz, offer devotees the opportunity they seek, since they are separated from the California coastline by several hundred miles and the Sierra Nevada Mountains.

Maine divers use rubber suits the year round along the rugged coastline. Minnesota has over ten thousand lakes with visibility beyond thirty-five feet in some instances, and the Wisconsin divers have almost as many small lakes, in addition to Lakes Superior and Michigan. The Chippewas and Menominee Indians still spear fish from their lakes and rivers.

But lake diving is not without its dangers. Captain Cousteau and his adventurous crew attribute the worst experience of their careers to the quest for the water source of the Fountain of Vaucluse near Avignon, France. They almost lost their lives descending into the cave that, once annually, erupts and pumps water furiously for about five weeks, then slackens.

Lake bottoms, with some exception, are muddy, making visibility poor. Those that are clear are crystal-clear, like Lake Tahoe and others in Wisconsin, Minnesota, Montana, and Colorado. Some have sand bottoms. Mountain pools, usually clear and cool, make good subjects for underwater study. Sometimes, a beaver can be caught at work.

Fast moving streams with intermittent rapids and waterfalls should be avoided. The waters there are always turbulent. And if a fast-moving stream pushes a diver's head against a rock, the diver's head will crack, not the rock. Keep away from waters in which you cannot master complete control.

Mountain lakes offer the best sport, unless organic matter has made visibility poor. If a lake is muddy it's useless to remain there, since lakes do not have layers of water, sometimes clearer below than on top, as in the ocean. After all, it is the sediment of mountain streams, lakes, and rivers that flows eventually to the sea and sinks to the ocean floor.

Exploration groups are everywhere, inland as well as in the ocean. At Wakulla Springs in Florida, a group of ardent underwater divers recently claimed a descent to 250 feet, the deepest dive ever attempted at this fresh-water spring, according to its management. Members of the Dixie Divers Club were credited with this feat.

Some lakes and rivers are open to spearfishing by state law. Many are not. An up-to-date listing is not presently available, but it's wise to check the state laws before venturing into strange waters. Many of the fresh-water fish are spearable. Pike are distant cousins of the barracuda while the muskellunge, bandit fish of lake hunters, reaches a length of some six feet and weighs as much as sixty to eighty pounds in the Great Lakes and the lakes of Minnesota and Wisconsin. Carp are found in many streams and ponds throughout the country and reach forty pounds in some species. Chinook salmon, or king salmon as Alaska fishermen like to call them, weigh as much as 125 pounds. They invade fresh waters in the fall or early winter from their Pacific runs, oftentimes traveling as many as one thousand miles to spawn. The chinook is a wary critter, but spearable. He makes the best table food of all the vast salmon family.

Trout and salmon abound in forty-two states of the U.S.A. More than forty species have been classified. A ten-pound steelhead trout in the upper reaches of California and points north makes good hunting in most rivers. The multicolored golden trout in the Sierras reaches six pounds and is fair game in late July or August, when the snows of the Sierras have melted. The brown trout is the most scattered of the trout family, next to the famous rainbow. He does not run to the sea and can be speared in the East as well as the West. The western variety seems to weigh more than the eastern breed, although this has been a keen point of controversy in the past.

Deep divers can cavort with the lake trout, the jewfish of the lake regions. They have distended stomachs like the deep-sea fish Barton and Beebe have photographed through fused quartz windows of their bathyspheres. They weigh as much as seventy-five pounds, but the fifty-pounders are more common. These trout are found in the Great Lakes, in New England, and in Alaskan waters.

Many bass are fair game for spearmen in various parts of the country. The largemouth bass is found in Maine and through the Mississippi Valley. The smallmouth bass is almost everywhere from Canada south to Alabama and all along the eastern seaboard. The northern pike, similar in mannerisms to the barracuda, reach forty pounds and are found in New England, New York State, the states around the Great Lakes, and in many other states east of the Rockies.

The gars, flounders, dogfish, suckers, mullets, bullheads, eels, herring, and sheepshead are some of the popular varieties of fresh water fish and all are game for the underwater hunter. The lake trout, especially, are sought after by spearmen bearing artificial air. They like the bottoms of deep lakes.

Many states, however, prohibit the use of spearguns in their lakes, rivers, and streams, just as the lakes of Switzerland, Italy, and France are off-limits to spearmen. In those areas, the "lookers" are more numerous.

SUNKEN TREASURE

Sunken treasure, buried land treasure, treasures in the attic—no matter where or what it may be, treasure has a fascination that can drive mild-mannered men quite wild. What man has not, at least once in his lifetime, responded to a tale of sunken treasure? Perhaps from an old seaman's tale, a magazine story, a motion picture, or a book—we all somehow have a hidden desire to seek sunken treasures. Somehow, every time we see an old map pinpointing buried or sunken treasures, most of us will go pretty far to dig it up or hoist it—given the opportunity. Underwater diving presents the latest opportunity.

Promoters make a healthy living from selling treasure maps. I have purchased identical maps in Key West, Havana, Nassau, and Santa Monica. They're all humbug but are colorful and attractive. They make claims to sunken treasure ships beyond our wildest dreams. If only the "treasures" of Captain Edward Teach, more popularly known as Bluebeard, were exhumed from the shelters of Pamlico and Albemarle and the thousand other locations present day promoters claim for the bold pirate of the early 1700's, it might pay off the national debt.

But even when nothing is found—and that's the case with the majority of treasure rovers today—it's fun for them. Every last one of the seekers is a walking encyclopedia of pirate lore and pirate treasures. The basic facts are that the turn of the eighteenth century saw pirates freely patrolling the seas in search of Spanish, English, Dutch, and Portuguese ships. The colonist's ships and ports were likewise attacked and sacked. Gold, silver, and gems were stolen. Somewhere, say the experts, lie the treasures. And anyone with time on his hands, and the money to equip an expedition, can outfit an underwater survey party.

Today's underwater gear, principally the self-contained artificial breathing devices, make outfitting and diving for treasures a simple and inexpensive adventure. Lungs have replaced expensive deep-water suit diving that once required large boats with decompression chambers and high maintenance and operation costs. Furthermore, lungs offer freedom and maneuverability unattainable by suited divers.

Let's look at a typical expedition in stages of preparation. Target: a reported sunken bark of Spanish origin off the coast of Summerland Key in the lower reaches of the Florida Keys. The channel waters are suitable for deep draft navigation. Therefore, it is possible that a pirate ship might have attacked a Spanish treasure ship enroute from Havana to Spain. Outside the reef is Hawks Channel, which affords a northerly passage with a six knot free ride in the Gulf Stream. Inside the reef, Niles Channel affords sufficient draft for overnight shelters, but a wary eye from the crows nest must certainly have been necessary, not only then, but now, too. Rocks and shoal waters could easily ground a vessel. Heavy seas could pound her against the reef.

Our expedition has a map—this one is authentic—handed down from saloon-hand to saloon-hand, guaranteeing the location of the Spanish treasure ship. Modern gear and youthful musclemen are all poring over both the old map and the Coast and Geodetic Survey chart of Summerland Key, Niles Channel, and two unnamed islands, mere rock piles offshore.

At the designated spot, the underwater men don lung equipment, masks, fins. They go down with knives, crowbars, and scraping tools. The bottom is sandy and full of coral heads that rise to various heights near the surface. Sea fans sway with the undercurrents. Sand moves about slowly and stirs easily under the heavy webbed footing of the marauders. The channel is about thirty feet deep, and in spots only ten feet. Fish swim lazily by. Barracudas watch from the distance.

The divers are seeking what was once a boat, no part of which could be evident today, for at least 250 years have passed since it was reported sunk. The wood has long since rotted. Star-fish and scale fish have long since eaten the trapped bodies of the seamen. Worms and bacteria have taken care of the bones. The anchors, and any other metal, including the treasure cargo, were strewn across the ocean bottom. If the sea was quiet when she hit a reef, or if the ship was hit by an enemy cannon, she sank quietly. But even when the waters are quiet, ships are at the mercy of the huge wave action under the sea. Ships are tossed about, underwater, like limp awnings in a hurricane. In stormy seas, they're carried about underwater for miles, usually ending up against a reef or wedged against rocks, there to lie until the seas digest her, cargo and all. In tropical waters, coral growth and plant life have a tendency to make anything dropped into the sea one with the sea. Growths cover up the invader, and before long—many, many years less than 250—it appears as though a ship had never sunk there.

So the divers have little to look for, except strange coral formations that could resemble anchors, cargo boxes, rudders, wheel housings, and boilers. Ships are never found intact unless the bottoms of that location have covered them up with sand, mud, volcanic dust, decayed plant, fish matter, and sediment—all of which act as a preservative. Usually such finds are deep below the ocean floor, and special suction hoses and equipment, derricks and barges, and lifting cranes are then necessary to scrape the bottoms to raise the loot.

The best way to search for treasures is to establish a bottom focal point and begin a circular search. Rope guides are helpful. As a circle is completed, the rope is extended another length until the area in question is completely scoured. Another very practical method is to use an underwater sled, a man-operated sled that is towed astern of a surface craft. The operator maneuvers turns to port and starboard, topside, and below. He can detach himself and sled from the tow at will. When such equipment is not available, a rope tow astern of a slow-moving boat will serve almost as well. A lung diver in mask and fins can thus search the bottom.

Days or years can be spent searching the ocean bottoms. There are many oceans and trillions of tons of water to explore. It's a healthy occupation or vacation. One die-hard we know has spent three years of book research and eight summer vacations seeking out a sunken brigantine. Together with a native Cuban helper, he dives with a Desco mask into which is pumped compressed air from a small compressor aboard a fifteen foot dinghy. He knows every sand particle, fish, and rock in the area and plans to spend another eight years seeking the treasure. He just knows it's there. And there are many others like him.

Frederic Dumas, an old hand at underwater diving and exploration with the Captain Cousteau crew, still has a driving urge to seek treasures. He once sought a million-dollar torpedoed cargo of wolfram in four ships that were sunk off the Spanish coast during the scuttling of the French Fleet in 1944. What he finally found were four ships laden with a cheap grade of iron ore.

The Mediterranean Sea, with its ancient sea routes, probably has more wealth stored beneath it than any body of water in the world. Before the birth of Christ, there was great wealth along all its shores. Empires rose and fell. Armies conquered and plundered. The great rulers as well as the weak rulers had their day. Much of the heritage of those early civilizations— the Egyptians, the Cretans, the Babylonians, the Phoenicians, the Greeks, and the Romans and Carthaginians—lived in a world of wars and plunderers. Much of the wealth of these empires has been discovered. Much, too, has not, and only in recent times have such treasures as the wreck of Mahdia, off the coast of Tunis, revealed the mode of life of their people who took to the sea. As time progresses, we will uncover more of the life of the early Mediterranean empires.

Our own shores share in the underwater wealth—but from relatively recent times. Wrecks on our shores, unless they belonged to the American Indians, are not more than 450 years old. Twenty, and in some cases, only ten years are enough to dismember and bury a wreck under the sea's bottom. But those ships that are preserved in the mud of the ocean could tell us part of our unknown history.

Another rare find in the Mediterranean several years ago revealed a buried wreck that members of the Undersea Mountain-Climbing Club of Cannes had found. Suction hoses exposed the wood planking of a merchant wine and oil-carrying ship of ancient times. When finally it is raised, it, too, will add immeasurable wealth to our archaeologists' knowledge.

The tremendous toll of lost ships mounts. Thousands of registered ships are lost annually the world over. Many of these ships are lost at sea, in water too deep for even modern salvage equipment. But in waters not exceeding two hundred feet, underwater divers with lung equipment can reach them.

The one disheartening fact about finding sunken treasure is that, in the majority of cases, it will not remain long with its finder. Claims to the treasure will pop up by the chestful. Government claims will pit one country against another. Our own government will enter the fray with tax claims. If the finder survives the litigation—fraudulent as well as rightful claims—he will probably never seek a sunken treasure again.

The professional undersea treasure hunter should have, as a permanent member of his staff, a capable attorney, to swing into action when a treasure is found. The recommended method is to locate the treasure, estimate its content and approximate value, then drop it. Leave it lie. If it has lain for a century, more or less, it will lie another few weeks, months, and even years. The procedure is to locate probable owners and establish which governments are concerned. The finder's attorney is now in a good position to bargain. He can get disclaimers for a small fraction of what might have to be turned over after the treasure is brought to surface. He can even bargain with foreign governments. It is doubtful if our own government will bargain for a bushelful of gold. But if the finder insists on revealing and bringing forth the cache, then he will surely be subject to taxes—and trouble. The amount of taxes? It's much easier to take a representative of the Bureau of Internal Revenue on the expedition.

The silver bar that came to light in the Bahamas several years ago is a case in point. There was so much litigation of ownership that the finders realized nothing more than discoverer acknowledgement. They turned the bar over to the Bahamian government, which has it on exhibition today.

Diving for treasure is sport and adventure of great appeal, one that most divers can easily be talked into. The lure is strong. And all this excitement will not be lessened until every diver has had at least one fling at treasure hunting.

I remember one expedition I was talked into. It lasted for six weeks in Bahamian waters, reaching almost to the northern shores of Haiti and the northeast of Cuba. For six weeks we plowed through choppy seas of Crooked Island, the Samana Cay, Acklins Island, Mayaguana, Rum Cay, and other islands. We talked to many native fishermen who had heard rumors of cannon in certain waters. Finally, we located one man who knew exactly where the cannon lay. For a percentage of the find, he agreed to take us to the sunken ship. He marked the spot and we dove. All we saw that day were barracudas and angel fish. Our reward—lots of skin diving and a glorious tan.

Expeditions for sunken treasure are always making news. From the southern coast of Spain last fall came word that an American salvage party was attempting to find the much-sought-after galleons scuttled or sunk in Vigo Bay by Don Manuel de Velasco in 1702, when he was being hotly pursued by Dutch and British gunboats. The ships that went down contained gold and silver bars, which represented months of mining in Mexico. Preliminary dives were planned by members of the expedition wearing artificial breathing devices. Big suction hoses and heavy equipment will follow-up their findings, sifting the bottom where the treasure cargo ships are supposed to be lying.

A still more ancient Spanish ship is being sought in Scottish waters, near the island of Tobermory. This one, the famous galleon *Duque de Florencia*, sunk with the Spanish Armada of 1588, is reported to contain thirty million ducats and the original crown of King Phillip II. Salvage from what is believed to be the ship in question was brought to the surface by the Duke of Argyll, a patient treasure explorer who has been searching for five years for the famous Armada galleon.

Remains of the old sailing ships must, in most cases, be unearthed by digging into the mud and sand. Fish skeletons, animal and plant life, algae, coral growths, mud, and decayed compositions have long since covered most of these wrecks beyond recognition. Occasionally, some metal remains—an anchor, a lead keel, a boiler, or tools are found in crusted layers of coral sand.

Exactly such a case came to light in 1954, when part-time explorer Edwin Link, together with an amateur crew, found an anchor midway between Point Picolet and Cape Hatien, off the coast of Haiti. After much research into the location of the wreck of the *Santa Maria*, the flagship of Christopher Columbus, reported to have gone aground on a reef off Haiti 464 years ago, Link felt assured this anchor was from the historic ship. From twelve feet of water the anchor was raised, a hand-forged model later identified as of the Columbian period, encrusted with 1¼ inches of coral sand. After two years of intensive study into the works of historian Samuel Eliot Morrison, most widely-recognized American authority on Columbus, Link, his wife, and his party were more hopeful that an important chapter of American history can be closed with this find.

Valuable finds of this nature are not too rare, but they are difficult to locate and often inaccessible. Coral growths cover remains of ships so skillfully that the most experienced eyes are oftentimes fooled in identification of underwater objects.

Wreck exploration, wherever the waters, is dangerous at best, but intriguing as well. The appeal of exploring such wrecked vessels is the most challenging of all underwater activity. Seeing a wreck lying on its side, or on its funnels or super-structure, keel up, should give a diver goose-pimples, and eagerness to dive into her immediately. Here is a dead ship. A hole torn in her bow below the waterline by crashing into a rock or reef—or a hole as big as a submarine, amidship, made by a torpedo during one of the recent wars—all these are intriguing underwater sights. Or she could have been scuttled like so many of the French Fleet in the harbor of Toulon that evening of November 27, 1942.

Depending upon the area and the amount of time she's been on the bottom, a ship is either coated with sea moss, barnacles that can easily cut the diver or his rubber breathing tubes, and plant and coral animals that turn the wreck into a phantom, or it could be clear of undersea life and vegetation due to short time on the bottom. An accumulation of shells and decayed matter could well cover a part, or the entire ship. Octopi and moray eels or scale fish are permanent inhabitants, depending on the waters. Octopi especially like wrecks. They seek the dark interiors of what may once have been a gay dining salon, a boiler room, or a dreary-looking hold—they all look the same to an octopus.

All ships seem gloomy and ghostly lying on the bottom. Anything as active and full of life as a ship seems out of place in the dormant world of the bottom.

A British bomber crashed, during World War II, in waters not too far from downtown Nassau in the Bahamas. The wing and a part of the fuselage lay in shallow water. We were skin diving in the area and located the remains, imbedded in coral-sand, partly covered by moss and tropical plant life. The trailing edge of the wing was some eight inches from the bottom. On the opposite side, where the leading edge should have been, were bare spars, the home of hundreds of lobsters. The shellfish had staked a claim under the protective wing, whose numeral markings were still discernible. Parts of the fuselage and other pieces were strewn in the area. We leaned over the wing and looked under. Lobsters were everywhere. They clung to every aluminum spar. We reached our gloved hands under the wing and brought out our dinner—six, 2 to 2 ½ -pound lobsters.

What is perhaps the most stunning treasure find in skin diving history has just recently been revealed. The place was off Bermuda, in waters punctuated by the hulks of hundreds of ships. The diver was Teddy Tucker, a 30-year-old Bermudian. The treasure was valuable and, even more important in the long run, of great archaeological usefulness.

Tucker, according to *Life* magazine, first found his wreck, which appeared to be a Spanish galleon, five years ago, and salvaged six cannon from it. Last summer he returned to the hulk, encrusted with coral in twenty-five feet of water, and searched for more. He found it.

In fact, after ten days of intensive diving, Tucker had brought up from the bottom a treasure vast enough to keep hundreds of skin divers dreaming and diving for years. There was an exquisite gold cross with emeralds, for which twenty-five thousand dollars has already been bid. There were eight other gold objects, two hundred silver coins, and dozens of workaday artifacts ranging from eating utensils to Indian souvenirs to a bronze mortar that still proclaimed through hundreds of years of corrosion that it had been made in 1561.

What had the ship been and when did it sink? Writing in *Life*, Mendel L. Peterson of the Smithsonian Institution showed how experts go about figuring out the answers and—having identified the wreck—use it and its cargo to study a period and as precise benchmarks with which to date and relate similar objects found elsewhere. Mr. Peterson suspects that Tucker's wreck was a French pirate or privateer that had preyed on Spanish ships carrying cargo from the Americas. He suggests that it was wrecked on its way back to France between 1592 (the date of one of the coins) and 1609 (when Bermuda was settled—settlers would have salvaged the treasure had they been there).

An interesting thing about the sea is that it preserves, for a surprisingly long time, gears and mechanical devices, and even motors. Mechanics who have worked on such motors after submersion claim they're as good as before sinking. But they must be immersed immediately in light motor oil before air molecules begin to corrode the moving parts.

Time and the sea, working together, can change the appearance of almost anything that finds its way to the bottom. Depending upon the area, the vegetation, and depth and temperature of the water, wrecks can live in recognizable form for a short time. Wood rots quickly and is carried away by the underwater currents first. Metals and superstructures begin rusting next. Finally, the ship just isn't a ship any longer.

Next time you sight a wreck whose keel is up, stand on your head, and take a look at her for real perspective. Enter her with care, for most everything will be floating on the ceilings, especially if her cargo is still intact and it is not heavy. An important lesson in wreck exploration is to be careful what you touch or remove. A companionway may appear sturdy, but one step on it and it falls in pieces. Anchors, lanterns, ships clocks, compasses whose captive alcohol keeps them intact, crockery, steering wheel, nameplates, and many other items are salvageable souvenirs from recently wrecked ships.

But more important than any treasure itself (which has an amazing way of disappearing in the direction of legal heirs, governments, and taxes) is to think for a moment about the historic and archaeological value of the find. You can't go wrong by first calling in the scientists of the Smithsonian Institution in Washington, D.C. or those from the Museum of Natural History in New York. You may not get any cash for your treasure, but you can almost bet on getting your name on a brass plaque in the museum.

Perhaps one of the most salvageable and most sought after sunken cargos lies off the coast of Brisbane, Australia. In 1890 *The Scottish Prince*, according to the Reuters press association, sank about one-quarter mile off the coast of Australia, about sixty miles from Brisbane. Its cargo of some one thousand tons was mostly Scotch whiskey. A group of local skin divers are searching for the sunken cargo—easily a vintage cargo.

A gallant chapter of rescue at sea was written into the legends of the cold, calculating Atlantic late in the evening of Wednesday, July 25, 1956. The episode—one that aroused some of the world from its sleep and met others as they awakened from a night of slumber—began with a violent crash at sea several miles offshore of Nantucket Island.

Italy's pride of the sealanes, the *Andrea Doria*, was struck a mortal blow below the bridge, fully three quarters through her superstructure, by the equally proud *Stockholm*, Sweden's luxury liner. The blow came at 11:22 P.M.; and exactly ten hours and forty-one minutes later, at the same Lat. 40:30 N., Long. 69:53 W., the no longer proud Italian liner rolled over on her side to reveal her screws as she sank to a watery grave in 225 feet of water.

The 29-million-dollar *Doria* loss was further dimmed by the loss of some two-score passengers—still a light toll for a wreck on the high seas in the middle of the night. But among underwater club groups the country over, divers gathered to discuss the drama that had awakened the people of many continents. Could divers reach her? Would free divers attempt to? What underwater currents would have to be fought? Could she be reached in the face of the oncoming hurricane season? And, as these questions were being pondered, two young men donned long woolen underwear, T shirts, and rubber suits—and strapped dual Aqua Lung tanks on their backs. The water was cold. One man was sure of himself. He had dived to 165 feet half a dozen times before. He was Peter Gimbel, son of the merchant prince of New York. The other man, Peter's friend, had not dived in a year and had

had only one and one-half hours sleep the night before. He seemed uncertain of himself, but he braved the descent and disappeared beneath the bubbles that still rose from the stricken *Doria*. He was Joe Fox of Bedford Village, New York.

The two took six minutes to descend, following the anchor line the U.S. Coast Guard dropped. One hundred and sixty-five feet marked the *Doria's* port rail. Sixty-five feet deeper lay the ship's starboard side, but Gimbel and Fox stopped at the port promenade deck. There Fox, who wore only four pounds of lead at his waist, fought the moving currents; he overworked and thus overtaxed his strength. At that depth there was 73.4 p. s. i. pressing against them—four atmospheres below normal pressure. Fox became nauseous from building up CO_2 pressure. Gimble came to the rescue of his friend, and together they surfaced in about one minute.

Fresh air revived Fox in less than two hours, and, before they surfaced the divers had made eight underwater pictures. They used a Leica camera with a French housing, exposing Eastman Kodak Tri-X film 1/50th second at f/3.5. They noted that the *Doria* had seemed grim lying on her side. Her buoy anchor was resting in a lifeboat; and other lifeboats, they commented, had worked free following the sinking.

The *Doria* will undoubtedly be visited by many lung divers in days to come, for she is in free international waters. Her treasures and the souvenir value of her salvageable items are looked upon as choice booty—for questionable Times Square souvenir shops are already peddling *Andrea Doria* "salvage." The wreck is not in especially simple diving waters. There is no protection from the elements—no reefs to form a barrier from the heavy seas—and diving here will have to be done in excellent weather—a rare circumstance in this sector of the Atlantic.

Already one life has been lost in preparation for a *Doria* dive, and undoubtedly other divers will be hurt. But this is the challenge of the free diver, for the lure of sunken ships is too great to resist.

PEARL DIVING

Another form of gathering "treasures" from the sea is pearl diving. It is not as colorful as seeking sunken treasure, for pearl beds are in known locations and are important commercially. Mostly, pearling is done by native divers with great endurance, who can reach the bottom to gather the shellfish from their beds and drop them into baskets. But from what was once a harvest of oysters for pearls has arisen a much larger industry—the pearl shell industry based on "nacre" or the lining of certain shells, called "mother-of-pearl." From mother-of-pearl we get buttons, costume jewelry, combs, and many useful items in daily use everywhere.

It is not the purpose to go deeply into this ancient profession, as it will not, in most cases, involve our skin diver. Pearl diving is restricted to certain tropical areas of the world. None is done in waters surrounding the United States with the exception of insignificant diving off the coast of California. The Persian Gulf, the Red Sea, the waters of the northern coast of Australia, the Indian Ocean, and some of the islands of the Pacific make up most of the pearling waters.

Native divers are nearly always employed, many of whom are paid a portion of their catch. They dive 100 to 130 feet on free air. Their descent is nearly always with a weight

—a stone or metal object held at their waist. They usually remain from one to two minutes, depending upon the ability of the individual diver. Oyster and mussel shells are pried loose from their beds and placed in a basket, or bags that are tied around the native's neck or waist. A diver, usually trained from early youth, can dive as many as thirty times per day, and aboard each of the pearling ships are several divers.

The nacreous lining of the inner shell determines the color of the pearl, which can be white, cream, black, or rose. Principally, the health of the mollusk and the varieties of chemical and mineral deposits in the surrounding waters determine the colors and condition of the pearls. Pearls, too, are not always round. Baroque pearls are irregular in shape, like peas, while others, as the blister pearls, are shaped like the dome of some of our state capitol buildings. But all pearls are the outgrowth of a foreign invader burrowing into the shell of the mollusk. A grain of sand or a parasite works its way into the shells, and the fine membrane of the mollusk will coat the foreign body with layer after layer of thin nacre, thus beginning the formation of the pearl. The chemical composition is calcium carbonate, a soft version secreted by the mollusk.

During the war, members of the armed forces practiced diving with natives in the Pacific who searched for pearls. Reports filtered through that some soldiers dove to sixty and seventy feet. For inexperienced divers, this is an excellent dive.

American expeditions have since invaded the Red Sea, the Persian Gulf, and other areas in the Near and Far East where pearling has, for centuries, flourished. Japanese divers, including women, are excellent. Japanese fleets, since World

War II, have invaded the waters of the north Australian coastline, diving for pearls and mother-of-pearl.

The dangers of pearling are many. For those western divers who descend in suit and helmet, the most feared of all are unexpected high winds and storms. Manta ray is the most feared fish, because its powerful wings can very easily cut the life lines.

HARBOR SALVAGE AND BOAT SCRAPING

The urge to put diving techniques to useful work is natural. Once the diver has mastered the fundamentals, he naturally seeks a specialty.

Today's lung equipment has given rise to what is a new commercial venture for some divers, and a combination of sport and business to others.

Some boat yards have, as part of their equipment, artificial breathing devices which staff members use for inspection of boat bottoms and for repairs. This precludes, at times, the necessity of hauling the boat. Many boat owners, too, own lungs that they themselves use to scrape barnacles from the keel, or in making underwater repairs.

A routine repair job can take on added interest underwater. Off Cardenas, in the northern waters of Cuba, a boat owner was repairing a loose propeller that had jammed against a reef. His mate, who did not have a lung, was skin diving, alternately holding the piston shaft and handing the Captain his tools. The skipper reached out for a wrench that the mate had been holding, but no wrench was there. Instead of the mate and the stilson, he touched the barbels of a ten-foot nurse shark, which had glided noiselessly to the scene to watch the work. He looked into the short blunt head and screamed. The shark turned tail and swam away.

Some enterprising owners of lung equipment advertise in local newspapers and on marine bulletin boards, offering their services to boat owners and fishermen. They retrieve anchors, outboard motors, diamond rings, wrist watches, fishing gear— or most anything. They assist the local and state police in dragging the bottom of harbors, rivers, and lakes for bodies and discarded weapons.

In Bahamian waters, a boatload of divers with lung equipment sailed to a distant out-island to salvage the lead from a sunken keel. More than forty tons of lead lay in five fathoms of water. A native fisherman had discovered the keel and reported it. He shared in the salvage operation, which took six divers who worked for eight weeks in relays, using two two-man saws. The lead was brought up in chunks of forty and fifty pounds.

Divers are easily earning the cost of their equipment. One large salvage job, or a steady series of jobs, will net a tidy profit, as in the case of a student in Florida who paid for his college expenses by diving for valuables in Biscayne Bay. He got his business by making a regular canvass of the charter fleet and the many boat yards in the local waters.

Another enterprising lad in the San Francisco Bay area cornered the underwater photo business, available from insurance and marine underwriters, police, and other agencies. He photographed boat wrecks, autos that jumped the safety rails on piers and bridges, and damaged rudders or propellers on private yachts.

Harbor work, however, is dangerous. Most harbors are filthy, cluttered with debris. Bottoms are a tangled mass of junked automobiles, barrels and oil drums, wrecked small boats, garbage, broken glass, cans by the millions, and mud. Mud is the chief problem found in inshore waters—harbors, jetties, mouths of rivers, and protected boat anchorages.

Recovering items of value or photographing in such waters is both dangerous and unpleasant. Even in Nassau harbor in the Bahamas, one of the clearest harbors of the Western Hemisphere, salvage work is dangerous because of the dumping ground the harbor has become over the years. Air hoses can easily become entangled and cut on unseen mazes of wire or on rusted oil drums. Work in these waters requires full protective garb, heavy gloves and boots, and an underwater flashlight. The diver normally walks along the bottom, if that's possible, feeling his way through the debris. One slip and a diver can be in peril.

The sea has been known to reveal strange treasures. From off the coast of Miami, a diver one day hauled up a dime slot machine. The one-armed bandit was intact; it obviously had been dumped from a boat, for some good reason, in about seven fathoms of water. The finder immediately immersed it in Diesel oil, covering the gears and mechanisms before the air could start to rust it. On land, the diver took the machine apart and cleaned it, piece by piece. He then reassembled it and today, in the playroom of his home, the bandit stands—a salvaged sea treasure.

TROPICAL FISH COLLECTING

A new craze—and business—has sprung up in recent years. Hobbyists and businessmen have started collecting and selling tropical fish, which are replacing the conventional goldfish in homes and offices. Hotels, theatre lobbies, and restaurants are adding color to their public areas by installing large tanks containing tropical fish. They are colorful, intriguing, unusual in size and shape, and now, surpass the goldfish in popularity.

With nylon nets and glass bottles, skin and lung divers, in the tropical waters where most of these fish are found, are diving to the reefs and coral heads to capture them. Fish are plentiful in widely scattered locations.

Among the popular fish are the multi-striped sergeant majors who are everywhere, easily identified by their vertical alternate black and yellow stripes. Small black and yellow finned angelfish are inquisitive and are always within reach of nylon nets.

Rare and expensive are the fairy bass, a two to three inch purple tropical fish found in the Bahamas and Haiti, whose unique swimming methods mark them as distinctive. They swim backwards as well as forwards, can hover like a helicopter, and then swim directly upwards. The cubbyu is in the sergeant major family but with horizontal stripes and is also in high demand.

Somewhat larger than the tiny tropical fish are the blowfish, another tropical household pet. They inflate themselves when they are angered, and they have sharp spines that can prick a diver on contact. The multi-colored male guppies are other favorite pets—the female is grey. Tropical fish are plentiful around reefs that house schools of larger fish. If there's food and vegetation, there are tropical fish.

Prices are high, and many a skin diver has converted his sport into a paying business.

~~~~~~~~~~~~~~~~~~~~~~~~~~~~ **10**

The Camera Moves Underwater

THE TIGER SHARK was closing in on the diver. The circles were getting smaller and smaller. The diver became more alert, narrowed his eyes, and watched the shark's every movement. This tiger was at least ten feet long, the longest he had seen yet. Its jaws opened to reveal two rows of needle-sharp teeth. The shark's maw was uncomfortably close, yet the diver's knife still remained in its sheath, dangling loosely on his belt. He hadn't even bothered to unsheath it, yet he carried no other weapon. Instead, he clutched a cast aluminum camera case which waterproofed a 16mm Bolex.

The tiger drew a bead on the diver, and in a maddened rush that seemed like a two-ton dragline bucket plunging into the sea for a mouthful of fill, the shark headed for the diver's face. Sweat clouded the diver's face-piece, and his heart pounded like a steam engine. As the shark descended upon him, he tightened his grip on the handles of his aluminum box and with all the might he could muster, thrust outward with it, directly into the open jaws of the shark. The blow stopped the shark cold, momentarily stunned him. The camera case snapped several teeth from the jaws, and the shark's nose was smashed. It hurt; the shark's nose is sensitive. Almost immediately, the tiger did a 180-degree turn. Its tail whipped the diver's mask off and into the deep it swam—its pride and vanity undoubtedly deeply hurt.

The diver calmly adjusted his mask and returned to filming reef formations on the bottom of the ocean.

Does this case history mean that every undersea diver should have a two-handled camera case handy? Hardly, but at times, when a knife and even a speargun are useless against a ten-foot tiger shark, a heavy camerabox is a handy weapon indeed.

A NEW HORIZON OPENS UP

Diving into and enjoying the waters below the surface is in itself an unusual activity. It seems almost unbelievable to be able to take pictures underwater—an achievement that until recently was reserved for experts like William Beebe, Otis Barton, and scientists from places like the Smithsonian Institution, National Geographic Society, and Woods Hole Oceanographic Institute.

The cheapest Brownie camera with a fixed shutter can now be operated underwater, when just ten years ago it took custom-made camera boxes whose cost soared into the hundreds and often thousands of dollars to house the expensive movie or still cameras that were used beneath the surface. In less than ten years, underwater photography has changed in outlook and availability to the point where anyone who can dunk his head beneath water can now make pictures there. During this short period, more advancement has been noted than in the entire half century before, dating back to 1893 when the first underwater camera was developed.

Diving into unique beauty and adventure is itself rewarding, but to bring back photos of what few people have been privileged even to see—that is real achievement. Of all the millions of people on earth, only you have photographed your own portion of the sea or its life. You have made a picture that no one has quite photographed before. You are a true pioneer.

Digressing a bit, here is a quick history of underwater photography, based on an article by Henry S. Moncrief, manager of the Fenjohn Underwater Photo and Equipment Company, in a 1951 issue of the *Photographic Society of America Journal*.

1893. First successful underwater camera developed by French biologist, Dr. L. Boutan. The camera had fixed-focus and was held watertight in a heavy copper box.

1900. First underwater photos taken with artificial light. Dr. Boutan again directed this operation by blowing magnesium powder over an alcohol lamp burning in a submerged bell jar.

1917. Dr. W. H. Longley produced the first still pictures with external focus, speed, and shutter release mechanisms. The camera was a 4x5 Autograflex enclosed in a heavy brass box. The Carnegie Institute Station at Dry Tortugas, some seventy-five miles west of Key West, Florida, was the site for these experimental photos. The camera was donated to the U.S. National Museum in 1940. (Dr. Longley's book, compiled after his death from his notes, by Samuel F. Hildebrand, was published in 1941 under the title of *Systematic Catalogue of the Fishes of Tortugas, Florida, with Observations on Color, Habits, and Local Distribution.* It was released by the Carnegie Institute of Washington as Publication 535.)

1923. Dr. Longley produced the first color still-life pictures in the United States. Color in those days was known as Autochrome.

1926. Dr. Longley experimented and produced the first color action pictures, synchronized to 1/20 second by igniting a pound of highly combustible magnesium powder on the surface with a reflector held over the top of the powder. The light was reflected into relatively shallow water (ten to fifteen feet), which exposed fish swimming for the first time.

1927. There is speculation, according to the author, concerning the first underwater motion picture camera. Dr. Paul Bartsch of the Smithsonian Institute in Washington, D.C. is credited with producing the first one that could be focused while in the water.

1931. The Bell & Howell Eyemo, the hand-held camera of today's newsreel cameraman, was encased in a cast aluminum housing and was reported to be the first commercial underwater motion picture camera.

1933. A camera was constructed with optically flat quartz window, and was lowered to three thousand feet. It was called the Johnson-Smithsonian camera.

1933. The first underwater light meter, the Weston, an earlier model of the same meter still popular on both land and underwater, was successfully used. Measuring light underwater was a step in the upsurge in underwater photography. E. R. Fenimore Johnson developed the housing.

1936. The ingenius E. R. F. Johnson developed a motion

picture camera that has such novel adaptations as diver-operated filter changes, a rotating polarizing plate, and turret lenses. The electric power driven camera came to light this year.

1937. The first commercial still camera case (Leica) made its appearance underwater.

1939. Drs. E. Newton Harvey and Edward R. Baylor dropped a pressurized case with 16-mm motion picture camera to seven hundred fathoms and filmed small organisms for the first time at such extreme depths.

1941. Dr. W. Maurice Ewing of Woods Hole Oceanographic Institution developed a Robot casing with an ingenious ballast rig that would automatically drop, returning the camera with exposed film to the surface. Flashlights at the end of a twelve-foot pole would automatically go off on contact with the bottom. This camera was successful at more than three miles deep.

1946. Motion pictures were made with 35mm camera in 220 feet by Captain Cousteau, Frederic Dumas, and Captain Taillez.

1948. William F. Dudley Whitman of Miami developed the first transparent underwater case made of lucite.

1950. The first hand-held color flash pictures were made below 100 feet by Captain Cousteau, Frederic Dumas, and Jacques Ertaud.

In 1952 plastic camera cases for the masses at prices everyone could meet were introduced. Jordan Klein, of Miami, began producing automatic shutter cameras and cases in plastic for $29.95. He retails the same camera and case today, with film transport and shutter control, at $17.95.

These were the major developments in cameras and cases designed exclusively for underwater use. Most of the inventors and designers were interested in establishing a permanent record of life beneath the surface. Their experiments have made it possible for thousands of photographers to take their hobby below the water line to enjoy what was for years a specialty reserved for scientists and research institutions.

WHO USES UNDERWATER CAMERAS?

Interest in underwater photography bounces from children to ichthyologists, from grandparents to Smith coeds. People are invading the waters armed with fewer spears and more cameras, it seems. Every diving enthusiast who clicks a shutter on land is inquiring into way and means of waterproofing his camera. He wants a record of his first dive, the first fish that swims by, the first time he goes to ten feet, and he certainly wants his buddy to shoot a picture of the first fish he spears.

Photographers are a fanatical group. One looney photographer tempted a moray eel to come out of its hole so his friend could make pictures. He suspended himself not two feet from the eel's hole and made faces at the eels' ugly snout. The moray, finally tiring of the brave stunts, came out and obligingly snapped at his mask. The brave one surfaced—and later discovered his friend-photographer had managed to miss the picture.

Less enterprising photographers are divided into various groups. Children and parents are the biggest investors in cameras like the Holiday and case which sells for $17.95. For movies, the 8mm Brownie is by far the favorite. The case has rewind and shutter controls and sells for $49.95 without the camera. Parents record most everything their children do underwater. A comparison of the first dive and one, three, and six months later invariably shows marked improvement. Most kids are natural-born swimmers and divers, and a film record of it all goes into the family reel or album.

Quite another sort of photography absorbs marine biologists, the most patient men of the underwater. They will spend days watching and photographing the male sea horse fertilize eggs that his erstwhile wife has conveniently dropped in his pouch—where they will remain until hatched. The female is thus relieved of maternal responsibilties, and it is noted that the male goes through recognizable labor pains in the hatching.

Spearmen are about the most enthusiastic members of the camera clan. First, they spear their fish, then shoot film of it underwater, and later they pose on land with their trophy. Find a wreck anywhere underwater, and there will be a swarm of shutterbugs shooting away with everything from the Leicas, Nikon, Contax, Rolleiflex, and Stereo-Realist to Holidays. Most every camera is adaptable to the underwater except the unwieldy cameras using sheet film or film pack.

Professional photographers, too, are invading the sea—Pete Stackpole, Carroll Seghers, D. Rebikoff, Jordan Klein, Peter Gowland, Jerry Greenberg, Philip Nash, and many, many more. Most of the top photographers work as staffers or freelancers for the national magazines, picture agencies, book publishers, and for advertisers who want underwater illustrations.

Hunter-Wilson Whiskies was one of the pioneers who used underwater advertising to catch the eye of consumers. RCA Electronics is currently advertising underwater television gear in national ads.

Insurance companies, steamship lines, railroads, salvage

carriers, and other such companies constantly demand underwater pictures. Insurance underwriters want to see cargo and damage pictures; the Maritime Commission and the Coast Guard want to see how wrecks lie on the bottom in order to determine their causes.

Diving archaeologists usually want a graphic record of their finds. The treasures must be photographed in their original state. The position of a Grecian urn in relation to the direction in which the bow or stern of a ship lay can be minutely important to these men of science.

Underwater club members are forever making pictures of everything from fish to still life. Some of the advanced do-it-yourself addicts have designed cameras that are synchronized to their spearguns, and others with unique flash attachments.

Students of the sea are illustrating their theses with films. Professor John B. Storr, formerly of Adelphi College, took his PhD. in "The Study of Underwater Reef Formations," illustrating his work with a 16mm color film. He spent many summers on the reefs of the Bahamas, capturing reef life that had never before been recorded. He is presently on the staff of the University of Miami doing special underwater work on sponges.

Still another group of scientists has perfected watertight cameras that are lowered miles into the deeps, making automatic exposures with flood light from within steel spheres, or with electronic light that flashes automatically. Some of these films reveal strange fish, some without eyes, others with more mouth than body, and still others with headlights stuck on the end of protruding antennae. From this world of darkness, deep bottom-photography has dredged up sea life that was never before dreamed of, for many of the fish who live at extreme pressures cannot survive in shallow waters.

For the amateur, there is no greater fun than photographing fish at close range. Catching a fish's reaction—and fish have been discovered to have emotional facial reactions—is indeed worthy of an underwater pioneer. Returning from the depths with filmed interviews of fish means that you have on film that which only a few people on this earth have had the pleasure of seeing.

THE EQUIPMENT IT TAKES: YOU CAN DO IT YOURSELF OR BUY IT

Mastery of photography underwater requires knowledge of land photography and underwater swimming techniques, plus the special aspects of photography under water.

The first thing, obviously, is to waterproof the camera.

There are excellent watertight camera cases on the market for most popular still and motion picture cameras, ranging in price from $4.95 to several thousands of dollars. For the mechanically skilled, there are do-it-yourself books and manuals on the market, giving all the details of fabricating and waterproofing the housing. This book will not go into such details. There seem to be as many homemade housings in use as there are commercially manufactured boxes.

Housings have been made of cast steel and aluminum, sheet aluminum, wood, clear plastic, copper, brass, and rubber. The very variety indicates that the housing should be selected for the particular job in mind for the camera. There are watertight boxes for every camera and for every job.

More elaborate commercial cases today have an air intake

valve. Through this valve, air is pumped into the case to pressurize the camera to a desired depth. For extremely deep dives, some camera cases mount a small air cylinder beneath the case, which automatically feeds air into the camera chamber as it is needed.

Since underwater activity is a relatively new sport, we learn something new with each dive. Some cynics hoot at wooden boxes—yet cases of wood have been used successfully to depths exceeding three atmospheres (sixty-six feet). Others like clear plastic cases, through which the diver can see every part of the camera.

In using a Rolleiflex with the plastic case, for example, one decided advantage is that all mechanical transports can be observed. A diver can look into the exposure window to see if the film advance is working properly. An exterior control for the lens diaphragm can be watched in changing apertures. The correct focus can be attained on the ground glass by looking through the top of the plastic case. Other cameras, for use with plastic cases, work in a like manner.

The best housings are those that have external controls for lens aperture, speed, film transport, focus, and, of course, shutter release. In motion picture cameras, the best housing is one that contains an electric drive motor within the case to permit uninterrupted shooting of the entire roll of film. The most awkward and useless cases are those that require the diver to surface and disassemble the case each time he must change any of the controls.

American as well as foreign housings are popular with underwater camera bugs. The precision machining and assembling required to make the cases and adapt them to the many popular cameras in use today tend to make the cases somewhat expensive. Cases for reflex cameras like the Rollei-flex cost upward of $124.50. Candid still cameras including the Leica, Contax, Nikon, Robot, Stereo, and the Cannon can be housed for from $99.50 upward, depending on the material of construction and external operating features.

The value of pressurizing cases with compressed air is that, if the camera box leaks, the air bubbles coming from it will quickly show the leak, and the diver can surface to correct it.

Some divers like positive buoyancy for their cameras, while others prefer negative buoyancy. To attain the latter, the outer case is weighted, usually with lead sheets, plates, or bars. If buoyancy is negative, the case will sink when dropped. If positive, it will float. The choice is up to the diver. I prefer to strap a candid camera to my body. A surgical rubber neck and waist strap keep the camera pressed close to my stomach when not in use. With this method, I keep a Robot, loaded with black and white film, strapped to my body, and a Contax or Rolleiflex, loaded with color film, in my hand. When I want to use the Robot, I attach the Contax or Rolleiflex carrying strap to my belt and let it hang while I use the Robot. When finished exposing, I drop the Robot, and it bounces back into place.

One enterprising diver attaches a Res-Q-Pak to his camera housing. In case of emergency, he releases the CO_2 cartridge and the camera floats to the surface.

External view finders are supplied on cases. Some divers like to sight through wire viewfinders, thus composing their pictures. Other divers use no viewfinder, merely pointing the camera in the direction of their subject. They usually sight down the top of the housing. Divers who use 35 mm cameras equipped with wide or extreme wide-angle lenses don't usually use external viewfinders. The extreme angle of view (62.5 degrees with the Biogon f/2.8 wide-angle lens on the Contax, and 45 degrees with the 50mm lens) of these lenses permits great latitude in sighting.

The do-it-yourself addicts have a great variety of metals and methods of construction from which to select. Some have made, and used, camera housings made from their wives' pressure cookers. An air valve inlet and an opening for the lens, plus modifications for external camera controls, and the cooker is a camera housing.

Brass and copper are suitable metals and relatively easy to machine. Aluminum is a popular metal, but it is necessary to exert care in casting if the cast is to be non-porous. Aluminum also oxidizes easily when taken out of salt water and exposed to the elements. Immediate rinsing with fresh water will help prevent deterioration of this metal.

Housings for photo-electric meters follow the same principles as camera boxes. The most effective are pressurized, and have an external control that adjusts for various readings. Meter cases have also been made from pickle jars. These homemade assemblies are effective, but if you value your meter, stay above ten feet of water. The Mako housing and the Norwood M-3 meter retails for $29.95. Reading for all film is possible with it.

Underwater pictures can also be made without leaving the surface. An enterprising female diver from Texas, whom we came across in the lower reaches of the Bahamas, had a plywood box with a plexiglass face constructed with watertight edges. The box was clamped to the stern of a dinghy at about a 30-degree angle. The photographer leaned over the gunwale, pointed her Rolleiflex down into the box, and she made pictures of the tropical bottom as a native skuller steered her about. Fish would swim up to the box for handouts of conch that she dropped overboard. She would then get ideal color close-ups of the fish through the plexiglass.

CAMERAS AND LENSES

The underwater presents special problems in photography, with many complications of surface conditions. It is, therefore, recommended that the better cameras and good wide-angle lenses be used for serious work. (Sometimes the best land cameras are unsuited for underwater work. The popular 4x5 Graphic and Graflex, or any of the Graphic cameras, are unsuited for underwater work because of the difficulty of operation. A holder is almost impossible to change underwater and a film pack is impractical. All sheet or film pack cameras therefore fall within this category of impractical cameras.)

Perhaps the most convenient cameras are the automatic reflex and 35mm miniature models.

One of the better 35mm cameras is the Robot, as automatic a camera as can be found on the market. One outside tripper actuates all mechanisms. When the tripper returns, it winds the film and cocks the shutter with a spring-wound motor. The camera is ready for another picture as fast as a diver can trip it. About fifty exposures can be made on a thirty-six-exposure roll of 35mm film. The size of the Robot exposure is slightly smaller than the 35mm frame.

All 35mm cameras with fast, short-focal-length lenses are suitable for underwater work. And camera cases are available for most of these cameras. Since conditions underwater can be unpredictable and hazardous at times, it is necessary to keep equipment to a minimum and as simple as possible to operate.

Wide-angle lenses are useful underwater because you want to work as close to the subject as possible. The farther the subject is from your lens, the less clarity in the finished picture, because light is scattered and absorbed immediately upon contact with water. (The red rays of the sun vanish a few inches below the surface.) Vegetation near the shore gives off particles that absorb light, thus making the waters still less clear, which tends to 'fade' the background of pictures. For this reason, telephoto lenses are almost useless in underwater photography. The closer one is to the subject, the clearer the picture and the more precise the detail.

Wide-angle lenses have good depth of field, so it is almost unnecessary to focus each picture. For example, the Rolleiflex 7.5 cm (three-inch) lens, stopped down to $f/4$, has a depth of field at six feet of $5'5\frac{1}{4}''$ to $6'7\frac{1}{2}''$. This is not much depth. The Contax $f/2.8$ Biogon ($1\frac{3}{8}''$) lens, on the other hand, at six feet will bring in a depth of from $4'8''$ to $8'5''$ at $f/4$—a healthy depth with which to play in uncertain underwater conditions. Since the more effective pictures underwater are close-ups, this depth of focus on the Biogon lens will give a sharp picture if pre-set at six feet.

All manufacturers supply depth of focus charts for their lenses. Get a copy and study your latitudes. Some lenses have the limits of depths of field engraved on the lens barrel for each distance. But these will have to be memorized since in the majority of cases the fine lettering is not visible underwater.

Objects, fish, and people appear larger than normal underwater. The reason is that refraction is the deflection of a ray of light suffered in passing obliquely from one medium into another, in which its velocity is different. In this case, with air and water, we have two mediums in which the velocities of light are different. This results in objects that appear about a quarter larger than normal. Unless corrected, photography suffers and out-of-focus pictures result. A wide-angle lens with an extreme depth of focus will often offset this condition when the smaller apertures are used.

One very important element to consider is the glass plate on the case directly in front of the lens. All commercial watertight housings are equipped with polished glass, similar to that used in lens making. For the home shop designer, it is imperative to use a thick polished glass that closely resembles the lens of the camera that's to be used. Clear quartz is colorless and transparent, with optical qualities closely resembling lens systems. This quartz should be used, not the brown, yellow, or other colors.

Underwater photographers abroad are more inclined toward the Leica and Contax than most other cameras. Housings are made for them by many manufacturers. Their versatility, automatic film transport, and shutter-cocking facilities make these cameras simpler to operate. Wide-angle lenses for both are available.

The new f/2.8 Rolleiflex has made this camera the most popular twin-lens reflex camera in use today. It is compact and sturdily built—qualities that have made it one of the more widely-used professional cameras in the world. External mechanisms for focus, film transport, operative control, and releasing of the shutter are easily made for the Rolleiflex housing. A hood for focusing can be easily constructed and will neatly fit over the diving mask, thereby shutting out all distracting light that might otherwise prevent sharp focusing.

Condensation on camera lenses can be corrected by placing a cloth bag of silica gel inside the housing. And when coming out of the water for the last time, wash the case with fresh water, and dry it thoroughly in the sun. Open the back and expose its interior to the sun, but first remove the lens or cover it with a lens cap.

From the simple Aqua Eye rubber bags, which house still and movie cameras in shallow water, to the expensive custom camera cases that can go as deep as a man and his equipment can descend, prices range from $4.95 to $4,095.

The latest thing in the Mako line is the Shark, an underwater camera that requires no case, for the camera itself is water proofed. This system of photography may well be the trend of the future, underwater. The camera is made of plastic, and over the lens is a fitted, clear, optically-corrected plastic second lens. This does just what a mask does for a man underwater: In order for a man (or a camera) to see, there must be an air space between the eyes (or lens) and the face plate. Between the camera lens and the plastic lens is an air space, thus enabling the camera to make clear pictures just as the eyes see clearly with a mask. The camera has an external view finder, a handle with finger grips for steady handling, a rope for carrying, shutter release, and an external film winder. The negative size is 2¼ x 2¼, using 120 roll film. No inside air pressure is necessary, and the camera has been successfully tested to seventy-five feet. The Mako Shark sells for $24.95. Like the history-making breathing units, this camera is completely self-contained. It weighs only fourteen ounces. It will, of course, make pictures on land, too, but it is basically a simple aquatic camera.

Its designer and manufacturer feels that more expensive

cameras with fast wide-angle lenses could also be manufactured, not requiring waterproof camera cases. In time, the
camera for the underwater will be just that, a camera whose
film can be changed in seconds, without the use of screw-
drivers and other tools.

LIGHTING

Light acts mysteriously underwater. Light rays dance
magically through the waters, darting in and out like fiery
flashes. There is no controlling them. Wave action, too, un-
controllable and unharnessed, reflects the sun's rays the moment they strike the water. Sit on the bottom with a companion any sunny day, and you will notice the waves moving
with an even tempo. You will also notice the sun darting in and
out among the waves, changing light patterns on your companion's face and body, as though he were bathing in darting
light. Such light will cause interesting and mysterious shadows.

There is light given off from an overhead sun and light
that is reflected from the sand on the bottom. A direct overhead sun will cause shadows underwater just as it does on land;
therefore it's best to avoid making pictures at high noon. Sunlight on sand, underwater, has the same effect as sunlight
striking a bright sandy beach. The sun's rays are reflected
from the beach, causing the eyes to squint. But since the red
rays of the sun are immediately absorbed underwater—and
since wave action refracts light—a small amount of light penetrates the water for photographs at depths beyond forty feet
on the average. Nearer the surface, refracted light increases
the opportunity for photographs, duplicating the brilliant
sunlit surface scenes.

The deeper one goes, the less light there is, although the ultraviolet rays of the sun sometimes reach 250-fathoms. Natural light at these depths has been noticed by explorer Otis Barton in descents made with his steel bathysphere. Long exposures and forced development of the new high-speed Tri-X film will probably produce some results this far down. But normally, supplementary light is needed in depths below fifty feet.

Most identifiable color vanishes at fifty feet. Reds appear black, and orange disappears at about twenty feet. Yellows have been noted at about two hundred feet, but only faintly. The violets, usually a misty grey, barely penetrate to about eight hundred feet. All this color phenomenon is reaction to normal vision without the aid of artificial light. But saturate the depths with artificial light, and colors spring out of the darkness. All colors of the spectrum suddenly become apparent. Reds and yellows and blues shine out. The glare of a coral reef almost blinds the diver who is accustomed to seeing black at two hundred feet. Caves and grottos suddenly take on new color schemes. Coral glows and fish take on majestic coloring. Colors never before imagined at these depths become alive. If fish are able to distinguish colors (and we don't know yet that they can't), they too would be amazed.

The skin diver will normally not be concerned with the blackness of deep waters. Most present-day diving is done in relatively shallow water, where light is present in various degrees. Light for photography, exploring, spearfishing, and for all the other underwater interests is usually sufficient.

The light varies not only because of the amount of sun overhead. Underwater visibility is also affected by the amount of sediment in the water. Minute particles of one-celled plant and animal life, and billions of fish eggs, are all in the pattern of floating matter. Mud, volcanic dust, sand particles, decayed marine life, and offshoots of the living organisms of the sea all live and sink in the oceans. A constant drift of descending life and matter is forever moving to the bottom, tending to limit visibility and cut the light for photography.

It is not unusual to be diving in turbid waters where visibility does not exceed twenty-four inches. Yet, clear that layer of bad visibility by diving ten feet more and the waters at the new depth are as clear as those off Abaco in the Bahamas, which almost always offer perfect underwater vision.

Ask six photographers making the same picture what their exposure and lighting factors are, and you'll often get six answers. Each photographer exposes for a different effect. Some depend on existing light, while others like to take advantage of varying dark room liberties. Some like diffused backgrounds, others like them sharp.

In relatively shallow waters, most colors are present. But as one goes deeper the waters become more green and blue; both those colors must be filtered out. Yellow filters absorb blue, green, and yellow-green. These filters, in varying shades, are useful with panchromatic films, depending on the depth and the clarity of the water. Experience with films, lighting, filters, and underwater cameras will tell the photographer all he needs to know. It takes trial and error just like surface photography.

In color photography, the preferred filters—subject to the peculiarities of the photographer and his immediate problems—are usually the Kodak CC-R series (reds, factors 1.2 to 5, depending on selection), which best absorb blue and green. The deeper the tone of red in filtration, the longer the ex-

posure necessary—just as in land photography. The gradua-
tion of the Harrison color filters have also been used sucess-
fully underwater, for both motion and still photos.

Best pictures are made nearer the surface where there is
more contrast. The deeper one goes underwater, the less contrast of things will appear, both to the eye and to film. Filters
and papers, as well as films, can produce a certain amount of
contrast; but in going after contrast in films, as for example
with Plus-X film, the photographer sacrifices speed, which
may at times be essential. The more contrasting filters also call
for more exposure, which again sacrifices speed.

EXPOSURES AND METERS

More shifting barriers to the passage of light exist underwater than on land. A current of water bringing algae and
plankton or millions of fish eggs into a scene materially changes
the light conditions, requiring more exposure or more artificial light or, at times, requiring a complete change of location.
Wave action refracts light; the sun comes and goes behind
clouds. All these interferences have a noticeable effect on
lighting conditions that affect photography. Photo-electric
light meters are still the best method of measuring light on
land or in the water. But in the water, a waterproof housing
must protect the meter. Some meters are adaptable to the
water. The most popular are the Norwood and the Weston.
They retail from $29.95 and up.

How does one use a meter underwater? If you know the
ground rules, they do not change for sub-surface work. The
sun must be behind you. Readings on shadows from your body
or hand will give incorrect exposures among marine life, as

on land or in the air. The meter case to choose is one that has external controls for manipulating the dials. This is necessary because water conditions change from minute to minute, and it's well to take frequent checks of light, especially when changing from one location to another.

Many charts and graphs have been compiled by photographers, mathematicians, and students of the underwater. These charts show transmission of light in relation to wave action, surface light transmitted in relation to depth, transmitted light according to various colors of the spectrum, intensity of scattered light in various water elements, and many more equally complicated and confusing bits of information. Each offers useful information, but the recommended practice for the majority of underwater photographers is still: Get an exposure meter and measure the light falling on your subject by holding the meter before it. This, simple as it may seem, is the most reliable method of getting correct exposures. Only the most astute student and scientific observer has need for percentage-of-penetration charts in calculating exposures. A wave of algae can enter a scene unexpectedly on an underwater current and throw the scientific calculations completely off kilter.

Take the complexities out of this and many other activities, and people can enjoy them more, and have more fun doing it. One photographer we know in the Caribbean waters—an excellent man with a camera and spear—makes excellent pictures without a meter. Why? He can't read one.

Pictures should be slightly underexposed. Then, with inspection development, the photographer can compensate by overdeveloping the film, thus giving the pictures better contrast. In the majority of cases, too, filter factors will have to be slightly increased underwater since the same lighting conditions do not exist there as they do on the surface.

Cameras with fixed instantaneous shutters are effective in relatively shallow water. Deeper—about twenty feet and below—corrections must constantly be made to cameras with lens diaphragm. As the waters get darker, larger lens openings or slower speeds are called for.

Most underwater action can be stopped at 1/100 of a second. In many cases, 1/50 will do the job. Fish pictures need the faster speeds, but only infrequently is it necessary to shoot faster than 1/100, unless a diver is so fortunate as to be near enough to photograph a sailfish or a tuna, among the fastest fish in the sea. But to date, no underwater pictures of these lightning fish have been made.

ARTIFICIAL LIGHT

All waters, until recently, were unknown and unexplored. Their contents and inhabitants were wild speculation. When artificial lungs were developed, certain waters became as traveled as the corridors of a museum, where mock-ups are displayed showing life underwater. Other waters remained a mystery. In extreme depth, where the water is pitch black, artificial light was needed before men could see and record life there. Even at less than abysmal depths light may be needed, as along the continental shelf off the Atlantic coast, where there are overhangs of rock, and in coral infested areas, where natural light cannot bend to reach deep crannies.

There are three methods of artificially lighting a subject underwater. The simplest of the three is by use of flashbulbs in suitable reflectors. Electronic strobe light and photoflood lighting are also used, but to a lesser extent than flash.

Home-constructed photofloods are used with surface 110 AC voltage and are hazardous underwater. There is danger of electric shock, if the diver and surface personnel are not completely insulated. Sockets and wiring must be waterproofed. Likewise, power must be generated on board a small boat, in most cases with a portable generator. The output of such generators is not at a constant voltage, and a decrease in the voltage system would mean a drop in the color temperature of the lamps. If color film were being exposed, it would be high in the red, since loss of voltage drops the temperature, causing an excess of red. (This, of course, is desirable in waters below twenty feet since desired red rays of the sun are absorbed near the surface. But it is not dependable.) Generally, this light source is dangerous except for the most experienced divers, with an attendant electrician. Underwater movies that require strong artificial light must, under any circumstances be lighted by such means. But usually, such photographic missions have qualified people in the crew who are capable of attending the lights.

The most professional underwater photoflood lighting equipment is manufactured by Fenjohn. An extremely portable unit that supplies color-corrected light from a 1,000-watt bulb, serviced from a portable 110 AC generator, is a new twelve-inch reflector unit retailing for $145. It comes with one hundred feet of waterproofed cable, and its outer construction is of brass and chrome plate.

The world of electronics has invaded the water, too. Perhaps the most important contribution to electronic lighting of underwater scenes has come from the research laboratories of Dr. Harold E. Edgerton of the firm of Edgerton, Germeshausen, & Grier, Inc., of Boston, Mass. He and other scientists

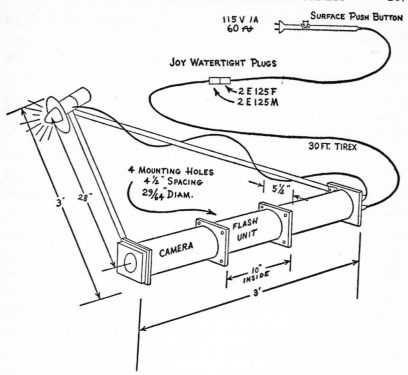

RECYCLE TIME ~ 10 SEC.
~ 6 SEC. (INTERMITTENT)
FILM ~ 100 FT. 35 MM. 800 EXPOSURES
SHUTTER TIME ~ 1/100 SEC. X SYNC.
FLASH ~ 100 WS. 2,200 BCPS
DEPTH ~ 1,000 FT.

H. EDGERTON

E. G. & G. Underwater Flash Camera, Type 222F, Push-Button AC Power

have produced practical electronic gear, which, he indicates, is constantly being improved upon as experiments and assignments with it are being conducted.

Since the electronic flash units operate on currents in excess of nine hundred volts, they must be perfectly insulated to protect the divers. Exposure to such currents in water spells instant electrocution.

The Edgerton units resemble long, capped pipes. In fact, the outer sleeves are heavy pipes of stainless steel, encasing the electronic tube, operated by both wet and dry batteries depending upon the type of recycling, camera, wiring, and where the camera is located in the sleeve.

Dr. Edgerton has been experimenting with a new underwater camera and electronic light, which will soon be on the market. Its principle is instant photo control when the constant A.C. circuit is interrupted from a surface push button. The unit is three feet long and 5½ inches in diameter (OD). The camera units and flash equipment are all enclosed within the sleeve. The lamp is mounted on the camera end of the sleeve, three feet above the lens, and held by an "A" frame bracket fastened to the rear of the sleeve. It is a ten-second recycling unit, and the flash output is 100 watt-seconds, about the same lumen output as a GE #5 flashbulb. The lens is an f/2.8 50mm Leica. Eight hundred exposures can be made on the one hundred-foot spool of 35mm film that is fixed in the fore end of the sleeve, the take-up spool being in tandem to the stock reel. As exposures are made, the take-up spool accepts the film and a conventional camera, as such, is not necessary. The unit is described as capable of working in one thousand feet of water, but since it is activated from the surface, there is no directional operation. The operator merely takes pictures at will and is able to make an exposure every ten seconds.

Dr. Edgerton is also experimenting with a new camera-electronic light unit, which, he hopes, will work in depths of thirty-five thousand feet. A special high-strength steel casing will be used, he reports, and the unit will be lowered to this extreme depth of the ocean at the end of a nylon line. (Steel cable, it is pointed out, cannot support its own weight at these depths.) This unit will probably have a light output of 100 watt-seconds.

All electronic units, whether or not they are combined with cameras as in the Edgerton equipment, must be designed to resist the hydrostatic pressure at depths in which they will work. At thirty-five thousand feet, for instance, the pressure against every square inch of surface of the camera and light unit will be about seventeen thousand pounds. The working tolerance of pressure testing should be at least double the deepest expectancy. This tolerance applies to cameras, cases, lighting equipment, and compressed-air tanks.

The larger the watt-second output the bulkier the equipment must be. Units with 100 watt-second output are capable of supplying sufficient light for pictures underwater. The conventional "slave" units are also adaptable underwater. These are extra light units that operate simultaneously with the unit of the camera, activated by a photo-electric cell attached to and facing the mother unit. The light from the synchronized unit flashes off the slave light and thus supplies more light, serving as an extension would on surface. Larger 200 watt-second units have an output of 1.4 per cent more light than the smaller 100 watt-second lamp, but adapting them to underwater use would be considerably more difficult, since they are bulkier.

Flashguns are still king underwater. Despite their decline in popularity on land in recent years, in favor of the multi-flashing electronic light, they are nonetheless more efficient. They provide better and greater amounts of light for the bulk they require than underwater strobe lighting. Batteries are generally enclosed in the camera housing. The lead wire to the flash bulb needs insulating. The tripping solenoid is generally in the camera, as in the Rolleiflex, Contax, and Leica. The reflector and socket are carried in the diver's hand or on elaborate extensions that extend from the camera housing and direct one or even three reflectors into the area being photographed. The diver changes bulbs himself. The bulbs can stand extreme pressure, especially the smaller #5, #25, and SM.

Offshore from Boca Raton in Florida, a photographer was making close-up pictures of some coral growth and sea fans. The bulbs were discarded as he used them, and they floated away with a slight northbound current. A cruising sand shark—not small, not large—raced into the scene and snapped up two #25 bulbs that were floating away together. He must have been an amazed shark when he bit them and found them unpalatable. But he remembered his manners. He circled back to where the photographer was working and returned the bulbs, all in fragments with dangling sockets.

The giant 3X and #50 flashbulbs, normally used for lighting ballrooms and similar large areas, are effective underwater for about twelve feet only. And then, the bulbs should be used on an extension, otherwise the same result as on land will result—the foreground will be over-exposed and the background will be black. Incidentally, don't go deeper than thirty feet with large bulbs. They cannot stand pressure as well as the midget bulbs. A second extension flash can easily be used to light the background. But remember, operating flash units underwater is not as simple as land operation. Water— and usually it's not mirror-clean—tends to absorb light as a sponge gathers water. Sediment in the water makes it more difficult to take advantage of all the light in your bulbs. Therefore, guide numbers recommended by flashbulb manufacturers are useless. It's best, however, to avoid learning another method of computing exposures. So use the guide number, but in underwater pictures, double the exposure by doubling the aperture opening. In some cases, when water is turbid or when there is low visibility, treble the exposure. This applies to black and white photography. Color exposures need more exacting computations as there is less latitude to color film speeds.

In color pictures, it's recommended to use clear flashbulbs, those recommended for black and white photography. Why? Clear bulbs give off needed red rays, which add to the flesh tones. But one word of caution when using clear bulbs on people—don't get too close to your subject. Keep the bulb at least six feet away or the flash will over-saturate your skin tones.

Another principle of land photography applies in the underwater. When one plans to use multi-flash, the best results are evident when synchronization is perfectly set. Two 1½-volt batteries will not flash two and three large bulbs in full synchronization with the shutter. Therefore, it's advisable to boost the voltage output with a battery capacitor housed within the watertight camera box.

Flashbulb reflectors cause more of a problem underwater. Since most camera lenses are wide-angle, the output of light must have an angle of reflection equal to the angle of view of the lens. In a 1⅜" lens, the angle of view is 62 degrees. The reflector, then, must equal that angle. One cannot retreat with the light source underwater, for distance will only minimize the light output although it will only slightly widen the angle of reflection. Therefore, the simple solution is to use reflectors with a comparable angle to that of the lens in use. It's not criminal to use a reflector whose outer dimensions do not quite measure up to the lens. The outer edges of the picture will be black, and the subject matter will be more highlighted. That's all.

The contacts of flashbulb reflectors tend to corrode easily after continued use in salt water. Sandpaper will usually clean them up, but after coming out of the water for the last time, wash out all equipment in fresh water and grease the exposed contacts lightly. Before returning to the water next time, wipe off the grease and the equipment will last much longer. Salt water eats up metals faster than a blast furnace.

FILM

Both color and black and white film, the same films that are used on the surface, are used for underwater photography.

In color, Ektachrome, Kodachrome, and Ansco are satisfactory. The slower Kodacolor films are not.

Panchromatic black and white film is best underwater since it is sensitive to blue, green, and red of the spectrum. Orthochromatic films are not sensitive to red, and since the infra-red rays of the sun are so largely absorbed by waters, this film is unsuitable.

Most surface photographers are accustomed to using one or two films to which they remain loyal. Underwater photographers might well do this, too. Since there is little contrast underwater, and since contrast is desirable in a photo, it is well to select a slow film that has increased contrast values, like Eastman Plus-X. But the desirability of contrast sacrifices speed, which Plus-X does not have. Therefore, under poor lighting conditions, or when a fast action film is needed, Tri-X is recommended. Some contrast is sacrificed, but some of the loss can be regained by underexposing and then overdeveloping for higher contrast.

Slow working, fine grain developers also help to increase contrast in negatives, and they also tend to reduce film and print grain.

The newest film on the market today is the super-speed Eastman Tri-X, rated conservatively by its manufacturer at 200 ASA. Experiments by photographers reveal that this film can be used effectively with a speed rating as high as 1600 ASA. Such a high working speed comes about only with forced developing, and at such speeds, there is a noticeable loss of shadow detail, even in surface photography. Underwater, all detail will be black.

Although high film speeds produce less contrast, Tri-X film is suitable for underwater and is best used with a speed rating of 400 ASA. Thus, you take a meter reading using 400 as the film speed and develop at 68 degrees with D76 at fifteen minutes; or Microdol at eighteen minutes, D23 at ten minutes, or Promicrol at twelve minutes. This development should be by inspection under a dark red or green filtered light. Unless the photographer has sufficient dark-room experience to produce professional results, it is better to take the film, with careful developing instructions, to a commercial laboratory for processing.

The same characteristics apply for both motion picture and still films.

New roll color films have recently come on the market; the noticeable improvement is their increased speed. This means color pictures can be exposed faster than before, offering more depth with no apparent loss of color quality. Eastman is now producing 35mm and #120 (2¼x2¼) with a speed of 32 ASA. This compares with their old speed of 6 and 8 ASA. Underwater, this means, for the first time, color pictures can be exposed faster than 1/25 second. In fifteen feet of water and lower, increased exposures are necessary. With the old color films, this increased shutter speed was almost impossible. All pictures were made at the widest aperture, giving no latitude in depth of field. If camera focus was not exact, the picture was blurred.

With the newer and faster color speeds, photographers have much more latitude and they can increase their shooting speeds to 1/100 second. Properly-equipped color laboratories can also offer the photographer another two stops in their speed, so instead of reading the meter at 32 ASA it can be set at 80 ASA. But this information must be given to the technician so that he can compensate for the increased speed in the color developing baths.

A new Eastman color reversal paper is also on the market. It's reported to be a paper base, capable of picking up the full color register at much lower cost than anything produced to date.

One well-known photographer exposes everything on color film and from the transparencies, when necessary, makes black and white negatives on a slow, low-contrast sheet film. This method readily increases contrast, and if he should need a black and white print of any picture, he would have it. But he also has it in color.

The basic rules of photography apply to underwater, too. Films should be kept away from sun and water. A watertight container is required with sufficient supply of silica gel to absorb moisture—one that is easily portable is best suited.

No matter what film is used, whether on land or under the water, never expose a picture while shooting directly into the sun. Sun's rays are refracted as they strike the water, but the same undesirable results will be seen underwater when the camera is pointed into the sun. Learn to shoot with the sun behind you. Film cannot correct for mistakes.

SUBJECTS—HOW TO GET THEM

As broad as the sea—that's the range of subject matter for pictures. Most pictures are made within the first atmosphere (thirty-three feet). In tropical waters no deeper than ten feet, a photographer can find more subjects than he can use among coral, fish, and vegetation. If he just sits on a brain coral and shoots what passes by, he will be thrilled with the variety of pictures. Fish will come to him. Eventually, he will have to shoo them away; they get pesty. Jump off the brain coral and sit on the sandy bottom. Be patient, and before long little animals will begin popping their heads out from between the furrows of the coral. A Rolleiflex with a double set of Proxar lenses screwed over the regular $f/3.5$ Tessar lens (3 inches) will get tremendous close-ups of the little beavers at work and play.

For a never-before kind of a thrill, try descending into a hole, such as might be found on the floor of most tropical waters. The thrill of entering the blackness of what seems almost a bottomless hole will never leave you. Look up and you can see a faint outline of the sky, but you seem to be swallowed up by blackness. In a few minutes, your eyes will get accustomed to the darkness and you will distinguish lobster by the score on the walls of rock. A grouper or rockfish might peer out from behind his hole. Maybe a small octopus will be lying on a flat rock, his tentacles drooping, or moving about aimlessly. If a jewfish is holed up here, he'll be near the bottom. All these fish are splendid photo possibilities. Get a companion to swim across the entrance of the hole. Frame him in it and you'll have an unusual underwater picture.

Or locate a wreck, a real photographer's delight. If the wreck is of recent vintage, with the ship still recognizable, then it makes for perfect picture possibilities. Again, shoot a picture of your companion through a torn hole in the ship's side. Frame him through the hole as he dives. The edges will go black when you print it, making an unusual picture of a diver sailing through the water, as seen through the broken side of a ship.

Creep up to a sting ray burrowed in the sand and make close-ups of him. Lie on your stomach and extend your camera in front of you. Make a picture of the spiracles, the breathing orifices of the ray, as he's buried in the sand. Only the spiracles are visible, plus a vague outline of the ray. Then back away and be careful of the bony, saw-toothed barbs that are at the base of the tail.

If you're really brave, get friendly with a barracuda, using camera and food. Try a dead fish at the end of a fifteen-foot pole at first. Offer the fish, drop the pole, and make a picture. As the 'cuda gets friendlier, choke up on the pole until it gets too uncomfortable. A series of pictures of the approach, the gaping jaws, the attack on the fish, and the retreat would be a treasure. But be certain you have several associates in the water with cocked spears.

Like the diver who became friendly with grouper in Florida waters, any photographer can make friends with fish, provided you feed them regularly. Eventually, if they are creatures of habit, they will meet you every day as you dive around their reef home. You can train them to go fishing with you, but be prepared to resist their advances. Once you begin providing for them, you will learn they have enormous appetites.

Simply because divers find their sport in the water is no reason why they should confine their photo activities to fish. Children diving through and playing in the water are excellent photo studies. Try bringing a child and his dog into the water. The dog will not dive, but from below you can see how they paddle with all fours.

Subjects are endless. They range from action pictures of predators to minute fairy bass not more than 2½ inches long; from still life to reef-top photography; from archaeologists' finds to childish pranks—all these picture possibilities are available.

Advertisers' products lend themselves to being photographed in water, and more and more companies are ordering campaigns based on underwater pictures. A nationally advertised detergent recently went after a woman's audience by showing how the blades of a washing machine swirl the clothes around in their detergent. Waterproof plastic bandages are being shown to advantage on m'lady's fingers, pictured washing dishes underwater. And so the "hard sell" campaigns go underwater.

But while watery ads are being designed, there are millions of people enjoying all that the underwater can offer them—from just plain looking to photography.

Skin Divers Are Organizing

AMERICANS ARE JOINERS. Political, professional, social, fraternal organizations—what have you—gather a handful of Americans together and they're sure to start some sort of a club.

The first underwater club was organized in 1933. It was the Bottom Scratchers of San Diego, California, and was begun by Glenn Orr, a commercial abalone diver. The club's first aim was to get more abalones; secondly, it has a social connotation. Since then, the roster of clubs, according to *The Skin Diver* magazine, the first official organ in this field, has increased to more than 450 clubs within the continental limits of the United States. An interesting comparison shows that clubs were organized in France and Italy long before the Bottom Scratchers, and other clubs banded together here in the

United States—but total foreign club listings do not exceed 180 clubs.

Club activity in the underwater sport gathered momentum in 1950. Regional and national associations became active. Ralph N. Davis, president of the powerful International Spearfishing Association, founded in 1950, together with other leaders in this sport, spearheaded the move for official sanction by the AAU. In 1951, the second year of national underwater competition in the United States, the AAU, under the chairmanship of Davis, recognized underwater spearfishing as a new sport, and it thus became the first new sport to be recognized by this influential sporting body in more than forty years.

Since 1951, spearfishing competitions have been held in several regions, all aimed at the annual national championships. The popularity of this new and exciting sport has attracted interest from scattered individuals, club groups, and affiliated organizations. Their obvious eventual goal: representation in the next Olympics.

CLUB ACTIVITIES

What is the purpose of clubs? How does a club help the individual diver or groups of divers? Is it better to join an underwater club, or can a diver have as much activity and variety in this sport without becoming a joiner?

Most of us like to have someone to tell about our interests, and since this underwater activity is relatively new, there was, for several years, a real lack of companionship for its devotees —people with a ready understanding and knowledge of the sport. The one answer was to join a lot of divers in common bond, if only so they could talk to each other. Now they have ways of finding friends and neighbors who understand their infatuation and who are in complete sympathy with it.

There is also safety in numbers, in this sport in particular. To dive alone is foolhardy. For years, the scarcity of skin divers made it difficult to find the necessary companion for a dip to the ocean's bottom. Today that situation is no longer true, and even in remote fresh-water areas like Emerald Bay of Lake Tahoe, Nevada, where visibility exceeds sixty feet, diving clans are organized for forays.

In addition to combining their interests and activities, most club members take a serious attitude toward their sport. Fish conservation is a major item on the agenda for most local clubs. With this approach in common, clubs and organizations of regional clubs rally against legislative groups with unified strength, in an attempt to show that the underwater man is not necessarily a spear-happy guy who kills fish indiscriminately, just for the joy of killing. The clubs have sensible outlooks toward conservation, often with self-imposed rules that prohibit their members from killing certain non-edible fish, and at the same time, limit number of fish or poundage in other cases.

"Operation Starmop" is still a conversation piece along the California coast. The coastline was being invaded by starfish, scavengers and enemies of shellfish. Shellfish are an important food fish, and also serve as food for scale fish; starfish are useless scavengers. Underwater club members along the entire coastline lined the shores one day to hunt starfish. Tons and tons of the marauders were piled high on all shores, a testimonial to the usefulness of skin divers when they are organized and given a job to do.

Most members carefully enforce club rulings on sportsmanlike behavior at all times. They establish their own rules and they police their own memberships. Some clubs insist on fines for any infraction of the rules.

Town boards, police, and fire departments in scattered localities have often come to local underwater clubs for pointers on rescue operations in the water. The popularity of underwater diving with the coming of each new summer has led far-sighted city governments to spearhead safety programs through the underwater clubs and their members. This instruction in water safety, equipment operation, and general regard for life in an unusual environment has been responsible for saving the lives of many amateurs.

Other clubs have offered their services to local as well as national fish and game conserving agencies, to state conservation societies, to local boards of health, and to oceanography institutes, for purposes of research on underwater life and conditions.

The Council of Diving Clubs of California, a Southern California organization, has as its prerequisite for membership a program of underwater safety that all must subscribe to. The council is active in establishing representation in behalf of legislative action. The members join to evaluate new equipment, pooling their opinions and reporting on dangerous gear or practices. The council is represented on the California Wildlife federation, a statewide federation of sportsmen's councils affiliated with National Wildlife Federation. This membership gives the council equal status with other outdoor sport groups.

Other groups and individuals have united to form the Underwater Explorers Clubs, a service organization serving in similar capacity to the Civil Air Patrol or Ski Patrol. The

IUSA has as its aims to promote spearfishing as a recreation; to distribute scientific information to institutions and individuals; to maintain standardization of rules; and to keep an attested and up-to-date listing of all world records for underwater spearfishing.

As a direct outgrowth of increased popularity of individual and club diving, the County of Los Angeles Department of Parks and Recreation has organized three separate courses of instruction for the skin diver: (1) Beginners Underwater Training, (2) Advanced Underwater Training, and (3) Self-Contained Underwater Breathing Apparatus. These classes, according to the county aquatic director, were begun to teach water safety and proper use of underwater equipment, with due regard for the increasing popularity of underwater sports in Los Angeles County. There are perhaps more ardent died-in-the-salt underwater fans in this area than anywhere else in the country.

But club groups have sprung up wherever there is a body of water. They are not only restricted to our coastlines. Inland groups with fresh water as their immediate medium are almost as popular as the seaside organizations. And members do not limit themselves to companionship in the water. Equal interest is shown in getting speakers, especially those who visit the United States from foreign countries where diving is active.

Homemade and professional films are making the rounds of club rooms. Members are keen to learn all that their fellow divers across the nation are doing. California and Florida divers are especially competitive—but naturally so since these two states are natural rivals. Members also pool equipment. Perhaps all members might contribute to buy the club's first

Scott Hydro-Pak, or the club might jointly own a still or motion picture camera that is available to all. In a body, they realize they will be more forcefully heard when local or state legislation is being considered that touches on diving. And they all know that in national competition, all competing members must represent a club, otherwise the AAU will not sanction participation.

Clubs have a broad range of activities. The Cleveland Skin Divers, for instance, are breaking holes in the ice of Lake Erie to bring back specimens for the Cleveland Aquarium. Ichthyologists there are researching cold water effects. In Oklahoma, the Tulsa public school system offered the Tulsa Divers the use of a high-school pool during the winter months, so that neophytes could get advanced training in the use of underwater breathing devices.

The Mid-West Amphibians of Milwaukee have mobilized their members in county Civil Defense and local police department alerts. Their time and services are offered as a community service, and in times of emergency, they will stand-by with the mobilized forces.

In Leominster, Massachusetts, the local Civil Defense forces have purchased a compressor unit for the Fitchburg Sharkmen, and this new piece of equipment rides along in the truck equipped with siren and red lights, which is used when emergencies arise along this storm-battered coastline. The Montgomery Skin Divers of Alabama were recently called upon by the State Highway Patrol to assist in the search for a man who drowned in Lake Martin.

In land-locked Phoenix, Arizona, the Sandabs have sensibly obtained use of a swimming pool where they practice, twice weekly, underwater safety and proper use of the various breathing devices.

The YMCA's play a very important part in water safety throughout the country. Since the introduction of underwater diving, many local chapters have regularly scheduled safety instruction, taught by qualified Red Cross instructors and local club members. In Lexington, Kentucky, the Mermen of Kentucky are a regular part of the YMCA aquatic program. They offer instruction, lectures, and demonstrations once weekly. The Mermen supply their own equipment and offer their time as a community service.

The Schenectady "Y" Skin Diving Club members have made themselves available, "to be more useful to the community," as they describe it, and have organized the "Tri City Rescue Service," an emergency rescue operation that requires diving into any of the surrounding waters.

The Long Island Dolphins of Flushing, N.Y., have mimeographed an intelligent list of *Do's* and *Don'ts* in the underwater, and a supplementary list of safety pointers with artificial breathing devices. This information is passed out freely in the metropolitan New York area to interested individuals or groups.

The Great Lakes Diving Council is an association of approximately twenty-five active underwater diving clubs with many projects. One principal aim is to get legislation enacted that will open certain of the lakes in the Great Lakes region to spearfishing. The association reports that the activity in underwater sport and observation is rapidly increasing and that divers find their fun in trout streams, pot hole lakes, and stone quarries, in addition to diving in the Great Lakes.

NATIONAL COMPETITIONS

Underwater spearfishing has recently joined the ranks of recognized sports. The regional and national competitions are now sponsored under the auspices of the AAU. This means that registered underwater clubs may hold annual competitions in their areas to determine the three-man team that will represent that region in the national finals. In 1955, eight of forty-seven AAU Associations were activated for underwater spearfishing. They were:

Michigan

East Coast Underwater Spearfishing Association (includes three AAU Associations; Connecticut, New Jersey, and Metropolitan Associations of the AAU)

Florida

Southwest Pacific Border Association

Central California Association

Pacific Association

In accordance with AAU regulations, all teams entering regional and subsequent national competitions must be non-professional. Since the Olympics are the goal of the underwater clubs, strict recognition of all AAU rules must be followed.

The International Underwater Spearfishing Association is the cooperating agency whose voice of authority rings out at each regional meet. It issues the rules governing the operation of all meets. Local underwater clubs are usually sponsors of the regional competitions, and they, together with national officials, police the meets. The rules for both regionals and nationals are similar.

All swimmers of each three-man team must be under the water, no artificial breathing devices may be used, and no other swimmers can be in the water to help a team member, except that each team member may help one another. Divers may come ashore and return to the water as often as they elect, but divers may not leave the specified areas of the competition. Chumming is not permitted—that is, baiting an area with dead fish in order to attract live fish—and each team must provide a float that has no motors or oars. Floats may not be attached to spearguns, and gas-propelled or detonating heads on spears are also not permitted. All AAU contests are judged by the total weight system.

Since national competitions have been in force, the following clubs have taken first place:

1950. Long Island Dolphins, Flushing, New York
1951. Southern California Skin Divers Club, Los Angeles, California
1952. Sea Downers, Culver City, California
1953. Muirmen, Pasadena, California
1954. Tritons, Miami, Florida
1955. New York Blackfish, Monroe, New York
1956. California Long Beach Neptunes, Long Beach, California

Competitions have attracted many clubs, and they are growing in size and stature each year. More clubs are joining the regional tryouts, and they are located in all corners of the United States and its possessions. The locales vary each year thus giving teams from California an opportunity to get accustomed to Florida waters, and vice versa. The tension at all national contests is high. Not only are the contestants vying for honors, but with each successful contest, the sport of underwater spearfishing, the newest and fastest growing sport in the world today, becomes more firmly entrenched. That firm recognition in the sports world is what the clubs and organizations and their every member are striving for.

Responsible for accumulating a continuing current roster of underwater clubs throughout the United States and abroad is a monthly magazine called *The Skin Diver,* devoted completely to the underwater fraternity.

The simplest way to make contact with an underwater club is to write, or visit their headquarters. Memberships are usually open, but in some cases there is a limit in accordance with its charter. Even when the roster of memberships is full, club members are always happy to have a visiting skin diver accompany them on scheduled club dives. The "Open Sesame" is usually a simple declaration that you are a diver from elsewhere, or merely that you want to learn diving with the local club.

~~~~~~~~~~~~~~~~~~~~~~~~~~~~~~ **12**

What It All Adds Up To

In the film version of the Jules Verne classic *Twenty Thousand Leagues Under the Sea,* there was someone who said, "The sea is a reservoir of nature, an introduction into the mystic gardens of the deep." Credit for revealing this wonderland must go primarily to the face mask. Wearing one under the water's surface is like recovering from blindness. The simple little mask has uncovered a civilization that has been lying hidden for millions and millions of years. Today, you—anyone—can see it for the first time.

The difference between land and the underwater is that our land, trees, flowers, lawns, and mountains are stationary. Enjoy them once, close out the day, and return to them tomorrow, and the same beauties of nature are still there, still enjoyable. The sea's objects of beauty are forever on the move, always changing. We descend into the sea for relatively short-lived glimpses of drifting plankton, which provides housing for millions upon millions of one-celled animals and plants, swaying and colorful gorgonia, coral that changes color when brought to surface, and the soft, sifting sands, which move at the whim of the powerful undersea currents. If we come to look another time, there are changes.

The many facets of this new-found underwater kingdom go all the way from coral to commando raids. In the past decade and a half, we have plunged into underwater warfare, with examples at Dieppe in World War II, and in Korea. Archaeological discoveries in the Mediterranean, off the Bahamas and off Cape Hatteras, in the Gulf of Mexico, and other waters of the world, have encouraged some scientists to re-evaluate their methods of seeking the hidden treasures of the older worlds.

Introduction of new equipment has brought museums and historic societies to reconsider temporarily-shelved plans to excavate known sunken treasure troves, since current methods and equipment make unnecessary heavy financing and large-scale salvage operations.

MASS PARTICIPATION IS ENCOURAGED

In sport, mass participation in this undersea diving medium is creating drastic changes. For more than forty years, the staid AAU had not entered a new sport into their annals of recognized competition. Yet they elected to write in underwater spearfishing as a new and commanding sport, practiced by millions, and enjoyed vicariously by millions more. In addition to real fanatics, the underwater is also claiming the weekend diver, a future challenge to the weekend golfer and the weekend angler.

The seas are wide, a non-exclusive club. They will accept all who choose to enter them. Even if one hundred million underwater divers elected to enter the seas at once, the seas would oblige them.

There is an industrial side, too. Fresh water has been made of sea water. Food and chemicals have been extracted from living water plant and animal life. Oil, gold, silver, and many, many other minerals and precious stones have been discovered among the resting places of the seas, or extracted from the water itself.

With ingenious minds and steel spheres, man has manufactured contraptions that descend 2½ miles into the abyss that no living man before has ever reached. We have conquered extreme depths—about one third of the deepest known hole in the ocean. What lies beneath that depth only tomorrow's diver will reveal.

THE FUTURE IS UNLIMITED

If the past fifteen years have shown such phenomenal successes, what will happen 150 years from now? If more than seventy per cent of the globe is covered with water, and to date we have only touched a small fraction of the waters, then what a future awaits the undersea explorer of tomorrow!

The attraction of the sea is undeniable. It commands millions upon millions of enthusiastic fans the world over. Most of them are anglers, sailors, and swimmers. The underwater divers are only the latest, but they seem to be more intent about it. They go down into the water and meet the fish face to face at their own level. Unlike the swimmer, who merely bruises its surface, the diver goes down deep into the bosom of the ocean, forcing it to move its crushing pressures aside to make room for this brash visitor who dares contend with the laws of physics. But with this man comes equipment that helps defy the laws of pressures, and tomorrow's man, with new equipment, will dive even deeper into the unexplored waters.

From taking home fish for dinner to merely watching little tropical fish scamper away at the clap of a diver's hands underwater, there comes a satisfaction that is unknown elsewhere. For the diver must rely completely upon himself. He must sustain himself with specialized knowledge and must battle unnatural elements in order to do that. He breathes packaged air in a generally unfriendly atmosphere. He must defy all the pitfalls of the sea. Yet he does this, and more, to enjoy himself in this strange world.

We can not yet call it quits simply because we have descended more than 350 feet in an artificial breathing device, or have dived on free air to more than 130 feet. And research does go on. Perhaps the most advanced research agency in the United States today is the U.S. Navy, whose underwater teams must constantly test and develop new equipment, which will serve them—and us—better. Most of their projects are classified, and not until they have been de-classified can their developments be revealed and copied for commercial use. Some of their masks, breathing devices, communication systems, and demolition techniques have been released.

Recently, the Navy announced a radically new signal device that can obtain an underwater fix more than ten thousand miles away. A Columbia University oceanographer discovered a natural sound channel at four thousand feet. Sound waves, at this depth, are reflected and directed along this channel. The Navy discovered that if a mere four-pound parcel of explosives were dropped overboard and rigged to explode automatically at this four thousand-foot level, the explosion would cause soundwave pick-up by monitor stations as far away as ten thousand miles. The station takes bearings on the explosion and can then pin-point the location accurately.

The Navy wisely keeps several Underwater Demoltion Team squadrons in active training during peacetime years. These skilled underwater technicians are a rugged group of young men who have every conceivable piece of equipment at their disposal.

The underwater fan takes to spearing fish, to photography, and to sport with ease. But in times of emergency he is on hand, too. During the Eastern fall floods of 1955, local skin diving clubs volunteered their specialized services to Civilian Defense, police, and fire departments. In Worcester, Massachusetts, where eleven inches of rain fell in thirty hours, flooding homes and streets, local skin divers massed together and evacuated the stranded. They formed teams to search the waters for victims. Their services to the community were a first for this type of combined rescue operation.

There will be increasing variations and developments, and deeper and deeper diving. And some day in the future an underwater diver may surface with a tale of the ultimate discovery—with proof that an underwater world actually exists, complete with people who talk, ride elevators, have children, in short, do everything that we do on the surface—and who perhaps go spearfishing on weekends.

Index

233